Risk Management: Framework, Methods, and Practice

Sergio Focardi

Caroline Jonas

Published by Frank J. Fabozzi Associates

© 1998 By Frank J. Fabozzi Associates
New Hope, Pennsylvania

ISBN: 1-883249-35-X

Printed in the United States of America

Table of Contents

About the Authors

Sergio Focardi is a partner of The Intertek Group. He has authored articles, reports, and books on advanced mathematical methods in finance and banking, and is a coauthor of *Modeling the Market: New Theories and Techniques* (Frank J. Fabozzi Associates, 1997). Dr. Focardi has consulted and conducted training on advanced computational methods in banking and finance for suppliers and major European financial firms. He holds a degree in electronic engineering from the University of Genoa and has a specialization in telecommunications from the Galileo Ferraris Electrotechnical Institute in Turin. Before forming the Paris-based consultancy, he was a director of Control Data Corp.

Caroline Jonas is a partner of The Intertek Group. Prior to co-founding Intertek, she was a senior consultant, Europe, with Regis McKenna Inc. Ms. Jonas has coauthored reports on advanced computational methods in banking and finance and is a coauthor of *Modeling the Market: New Theories and Techniques.* She graduated in political science from the University of Illinois, Urbana-Champaign.

The Intertek Group is a Paris-based firm specialized in research, consulting, and training on analytical and numerical methods in banking and finance.

Preface

This book was researched and written for persons with a professional interest in financial risk management. Based on conversations with 90 individuals from industry and academia, this book

- explores the theoretical framework of and methodologies used in risk management,
- examines industry implementation of risk management methodologies,
- identifies areas where today's finance theory and modeling are insufficient, and
- explores the research effort to arrive at a more empirically faithful modeling of financial phenomena.

In so doing, it traces the rapid development of risk management methodologies and practice as the accent shifts from control to optimization.

This book does not presuppose any knowledge of sophisticated mathematical techniques. However, the Appendices provide a summary of the fundamental concepts of mathematical finance and of new mathematical theories borrowed from physics and the social sciences. By contributing to our ability to understand and model the economy and financial markets, the latter hold the promise of better risk management.

Sergio Focardi
Caroline Jonas

Acknowledgements

Risk Management: Framework, Methods, and Practice is based on interviews with 90 persons from banking and finance, the academic community, hardware and software suppliers and consultants. We wish to thank the persons and organizations listed below who contributed to this book by sharing with us their experience and their views.

Financial institutions in the U.S.A.: American Stock Exchange • Bankers Trust • Bear Stearns • Chase Manhattan Bank • Credit Lyonnais Americas • Credit Suisse First Boston • Goldman Sachs • Lehman Brothers • Long-Term Capital Management • Merrill Lynch • JP Morgan • Morgan Stanley • Sakura Global Capital.

Financial institutions in Europe: Banca Commerciale Italiana • Bank Austria • Barclays Bank • BZW Barclays • Credis Fund Service • Crédit Commercial de France • Credit Suisse First Boston • Den norske Bank • First Chicago NBD • Generale Bank • Goldman Sachs • ING Barings • Sakura Global Capital • SBC Warburg • Société Générale • Union Bank of Switzerland • Zuercher Kantonalbank.

Academic community: Carol Alexander (University of Sussex) • William Brock (University of Wisconsin) • Andrea Buraschi (London Business School) • Freddy Delbaen (Swiss Federal Institute of Technology-Zurich) • Jean Dermine (INSEAD) • Paul Embrechts (Swiss Federal Institute of Technology-Zurich) • Larry Epstein (University of Toronto) • Mark Garman (University of California-Berkeley) • Robert Geske (University of California-Los Angeles) • Lars Hansen (University of Chicago) • Thomas Ho • Chi-fu Huang • John Hull (University of Toronto) • Robert Jarrow (Cornell University) • Alan Kirman (University of Aix-Marseille) • Blake LeBaron (University of Wisconsin) • Thomas Sargent (University of Chicago) • José Scheinkman (University of Chicago) • Ton Vorst (Erasmus University Rotterdam).

Suppliers, consultants: A-J Financial Systems • Algorithmics • Bankers Trust Raroc Group • BARRA • Capital Market Risk Advisors • C*ATS Software • Chase Client Risk Management Services • Coopers & Lybrand • Digital Equipment Corporation • Ecofin Research & Consulting • Financial Engineering Associates (FEA) • Global Advanced Technology (GAT) • IBM • Infinity Financial Technology • The Kamakura Corporation • KMV Corporation • JP Morgan Risk Management Services • Olsen & Associates • Quantitative Risk Management (QRM) • Risk Management Technologies (RMT) • Reuters • Sailfish Systems • SunGard Capital Markets • Treasury Services • Trepp Risk Management • Visible Decisions.

N.B.: Some persons may have changed positions since we talked to them. Reference is made to persons in function of the post they occupied at the time of the interview.

Chapter 1

Why Manage Risk?

1.1 INTRODUCTION

Risk management is different things to different people. For regulators, says Colin Lawrence, head of global market risk at BZW Barclays in London, risk management is about control, for traders it's a question of hedging their risks, and for risk managers it is allocating capital to obtain the highest return relating to risk. This book looks at risk management from the perspective of the latter, that is to say from the point of view of controlling and optimizing the risk-return profile of the firm. In doing so, it covers questions of how risk is quantified and measured and how decisions are made to hedge away unwanted risks and to optimize the management of selected risks. Issues related to both trading-floor activities and commercial banking are discussed.

Risk management is at the core of finance, not a recent addition to a long series of innovations. The novelty is the type and amount of risk being managed, the methodologies employed, and investors' awareness of risk. David LaCross, CEO of Risk Management Technologies, observes that risk — once defined as variability in outcome — must now take into consideration not only the magnitude (size) of risk, but also the nature (shape) of risk. This, he notes, is due to increased optionality.

What is risk management and where are financial firms in implementing it? Luc Henrard, head of risk management at Brussels-based Generale Bank, describes a three-step process that includes: (1) getting all the uncertainties upfront, (2) attributing a measure to uncertainty, and (3) optimizing. He considers that the banking system is now in the middle of the step 2.

There is risk because there is uncertainty about future events. The first and most basic concept in risk management is the definition of the set of possible future contingencies, i.e., the identification of the possible "states" of the economy. An abstract concept, this is the space generally called omega (Ω) in modern mathematical finance theory.

1

A state — or scenario — is a *possible* history of the economy over a given period. In practice, states are identified by sets of prices and rates at different points of the period, for instance, one day or one month. In more general terms, states might also be identified by sets of functions of time that represent the relevant economic variables. The term structure of interest rates, for example, is an entire curve over a period.

Financial modeling requires computing the functions that represent states. These computations depend on the type of model one adopts. Using a single-period model, the values of security prices are computed only at the end of a given period. Using a multiperiod binomial model, all possible paths of security prices are computed over multiple periods, assuming that for each period security prices may go up or down by a fixed amount. Using a continuous-time continuous-state model, the infinite space of states must be sampled.

Defining and generating a set of possible scenarios is not a trivial task: considering every possible contingency might result in an unmanageable number of scenarios. The modeling objective is therefore to reduce computational complexity by reducing to a minimum the number of scenarios to be considered, without losing important information. Only scenarios that are possible and representative are calculated.

Generating possible scenarios does not, however, result in a quantitative measure of risk. To measure risk quantitatively, some measure of uncertainty must be attached to the scenarios. This implies the adoption of a theoretical framework for measuring uncertainty. Probability — a rigorous mathematical concept — is the most common measure of uncertainty, but its application is often problematic.

The first difficulty in applying probability is the fact that most financial time series of interest in risk management have only one realization. There is, for instance, only one risk-free interest rate for each currency. But the usual statistical interpretation of probability takes an ensemble view of probability, interpreting it as relative frequency. As there is only one realization of most economic time series, probability must be translated into time statistics. Probabilistic variance, for example, becomes the variance of successive values of a time series over a given period.

Equating probabilistic expected values with time averages is a delicate mathematical operation. Stationary processes for which the equivalence holds are called ergodic processes. The concept of ergodic processes, itself subject to many mathematical subtleties, is difficult to apply if one assumes, as is necessary in risk management, that probabilities vary in time.

Typically, the assumption is made that over sufficiently long periods of time probabilistic averages are well approximated by time averages. This approximation cannot be justified rigorously and fails to hold in many critical instances. In the case of regime shifts, it is clearly violated.

This consideration leads to the second difficulty in applying probability: a number of events of interest in risk management are rare or intrinsically unique. In the absence of reliable statistical samples, these events cannot be the subject of statistical measurement and their probability assignments are difficult to interpret. They are, however, possible and need to be considered and, in one way or another, differentiated as regards the measure of uncertainty they carry.

Events whose uncertainty measures can somehow be ascertained through statistical observations must be separated from events whose uncertainty is evaluated through subjective judgement or theoretical extrapolations that are not statistical in nature. The two types of events serve different objectives and are subject to different rules.

It should be noted that subjective quantitative evaluations of uncertainty might not be well represented by the mathematical concept of probability. One might, for instance, be able to make a quantitative judgement of uncertainty for only some region of the parameters. It is conceivable to extend the possible logical representation of uncertainty to include a broader class of uncertainty measures of which probability is only one representative. There are non-probabilistic approaches to measuring uncertainty. One such approach — an asset pricing theory in a non-probabilistic framework — was developed by Larry Epstein, professor of economics at the University of Toronto.

Chi-fu Huang, formerly J.C. Penney professor of finance at MIT and now a principal of Long-Term Capital Management, remarks that while non-probabilistic approaches have been tried by academics, no big organization is using them. The classical probabilistic approach has, he notes, proved useful and is understood by everyone. While step-by-step deviations might be possible, radical moves away from well established concepts confront inertia.

This view is shared by Andrew Morton, co-developer of the Heath-Jarrow-Morton interest-rate model and now head of the analytics group for the fixed income department at Lehman Brothers. Looking at past progress and extrapolating forward, Dr. Morton believes that it will be a long time — if ever — before non-probabilistic notions work their way into finance.

A probabilistic representation of possible contingencies is a complete representation of risk. Concepts such as VaR are single-number measures that capture, in a concise way, the global riskiness of a firm's exposure. These measures imply the "collapsing" of information and reflect only some global aspect of risk. They are important because, unable to deal with the complexities of probability distributions, human agents need a summary risk measure.

Risk measurement implies that there is some model of the market that, when applied to data, measures risk. But risk management is not limited to the more or less scientific process of measuring risk. Once measured, subjective judgement is used to evaluate and make decisions upon the measurement. This is an entirely different process. Freddy Delbaen, who holds the chair of financial mathematics at the Swiss Federal Institute of Technology-Zurich, distinguishes between the description of financial markets, a scientific theory that entails the measurement of risk, and risk management.

Management decides the type and level of risk to bear and issues appropriate rules and policies. Prof. Delbaen decomposes risk management into three processes: (1) gather data, (2) apply models, and (3) apply institutional rules. He believes that, while today's models may be very sophisticated, not enough data is being used. The importance of data will be a recurrent theme in this book.

Prof. Delbaen observes that increased competition and the changing market environment will force all financial institutions, pension funds included, to take on more risk. The important question is "Does the global portfolio have a big risk?" The answer, he notes, is not just one quantity that can be called "risk" as in weight: some measure risk in probability, others in variance; still others use another measure.

Figure 1.1
The risk management process is increasingly guided by science as data and measurement play an ever-growing role.

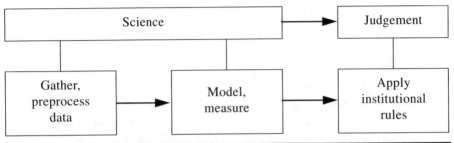

Though managing risk may not be a full 100% scientific job for a long time, Prof. Delbaen notes that common sense, intuition, and interpretation are increasingly guided by data and measurement (see Figure 1.1). Sophisticated probability laws are now being used; back-office models allow to check if traders are sticking to the rules. But a number of processes remain momentarily outside of the realm of science. These include the setting of limits, the "digestion" of the risk measurement, the definition of the firm's goals and appetite for risk, and the setting of time horizons.

1.2 THE OBJECTIVES OF RISK MANAGEMENT

The objectives of risk management vary from player to player. The over-riding concern of the regulatory agencies is to protect the financial system. This involves protecting investors, especially small investors with an information disadvantage, against unfair speculation by those who manage their investments. It also involves protecting the system against possible meltdown triggered by large-scale failures. Given the leverage possible in modern financial trading, protection is a vital objective.

Regulators are also concerned with questions related to the overall macroeconomic effect of risk management. How will firm-wide risk management affect the global risk and volatility present in the markets? Is there any way to protect against large-scale market swellings? What are the ultimate risks present in the economy?

There is the perception that regulators understand the basic process of value generation and the process of risk management at the firm level. But at different levels of aggregation, namely at the global macroeconomic level, financial risk is still poorly understood. There is no widespread agreement on the effectiveness of measures to protect the system; nor is there a sound understanding of just what the risks are.

As for financial firms, the objectives of risk management vary from one organization to another and from one function or level to another inside the same organization. Broadly speaking, financial firms have four objectives in risk management:

- comply with the regulators
- obtain a good rating, at the product and/or firmwide level
- protect the business against unfavorable events
- optimize the risk-return trade-off.

Regulators have introduced the requirement of the quantitative statistical measurement of risk. For most firms, this is a significant cultural change. Meeting reporting requirements is absorbing resources at financial firms on both sides of the Atlantic as they strive to produce a quantitative measure of risk. The big question firms are now asking, remarks Keith Bear, head of risk management for IBM Europe, is: "Are we doing this just for the regulators?" He observes that small banks and many of the larger ones are still managing risk across the board with spreadsheets.

Risk measurement reporting is also a means to achieving a good evaluation from the rating agencies. For some institutions, this is key to their business. To obtain a triple-A rating, S&P and Moody's require that a derivatives product firm have in place a unified architecture for analyzing both market and credit risk.

Farshid Jamshidian, managing director of product development and strategic trading at Sakura Global Capital in London, remarks that Sakura Prime, their new derivatives vehicle, relies significantly on accurate firmwide assessment and control of market and credit risk. For this purpose, Dr. Jamshidian and Yu Zhu, his colleague in New York, developed a scenario simulation theory and methodology for monitoring risk exposures and calculating VaR and credit reserves. The model was applied to Sakura Prime, which subsequently obtained AAA rating from S&P and Moody's.

The role of the rating system is likely to grow. With the diffusion of credit risk measurement, credit ratings will become a determinant of asset prices. CreditMetrics, a framework for quantifying credit risk released by J.P. Morgan, uses the rating system to evaluate credit risk and to measure how rating migrations impact the market risk of portfolios.

A good risk management system can also have a positive impact on a firm's image. There is a growing sensitivity to risk on the part of investors and market participants in general. For Jean-Marc Eber, head of R&D at Société Générale's capital markets division in Paris, good risk management is an effective marketing tool.

But risk management is perhaps first and foremost a control and optimization function. Methodologies used to comply with regulations may not be the same as those used to control and optimize risk. In fact, interviewees remarked that the risk management approach used internally by many major firms differs from that used to satisfy the requirements of rating agencies or regulatory bodies.

As a control function, risk management implies a quantitative evaluation of risk. To control risk is to ensure that, over a given period, risk remains within determined limits. If risk is expressed as a probability distribution over a given time horizon, criteria have to be applied to determine whether or not the probability distribution carries excessive risk.

For John Hull, co-developer of the Hull-White interest-rate model and co-founder of Toronto-based A-J Financial Systems, the challenge of risk management as a control function is to answer the questions: "How bad can things get?" and "What do you mean by how bad?" Typically, he says, the objective is to see 10 days ahead with 99% confidence. But answering the question "How bad?" is not so easy, Dr. Hull adds: it raises a lot of technical questions.

The role attributed to the control and optimization functions depends on the business one is in. In the derivatives business, says Yu Zhu, director of risk assessment and control at Sakura Global Capital in New York, risk management is primarily a question of hedging trades and making sure that the global risk is under control. A head trader might, he says, think he is managing risk because he is hedging. But for Dr. Zhu, risk management is managing global risk with fourteen different currencies including exotics such as the Thai. Dr. Jamshidian at Sakura's London office adds that, for a firm like Sakura, risk management is a control function that ensures that risk does not go above corporate levels once you have hedged away locally.

Controlling risk in the derivatives business is not a simple task. Understanding and computing adverse scenarios is difficult in and of itself. It requires evaluating events at the frontier, where statistical measurements lose meaning. At the same time, the consideration of exceptionally unlikely scenarios would require inordinately large amounts of capital. The complexity of portfolios with their many nonlinearities adds additional challenges to the control function.

In a broader sense, risk management is a question of the optimal allocation of resources: it is a financial optimization function. Its task, according to Dirk-Emma Baestaens, formerly professor of finance at Erasmus University Rotterdam and now head of R&D for credit risk with Generale Bank in Brussels, goes beyond ensuring that the firm stays in business. Its ultimate function, he says, is to deliver better value to shareholders. In a similar vein, Fred Stambaugh, global head of strategic risk management advisory at First Chicago NBD in London, cites as a key objective of risk management the evaluation of trading businesses in terms of return on capital.

Risk management as financial optimization might involve different time horizons. As a control function, market risk management has short time horizons, typically the time deemed necessary to unwind positions. As an optimization function, however, risk management might consider time horizons of up to one year.

One difficulty in the optimization process is that risk management implies, at the end of the risk measurement cycle, a fundamentally subjective management decision on the level of protection to implement. The trade-off is between protection against unfavorable events and profitability. But understanding risk-return trade-offs is not so easy. Pierre Antolinez-Fehr, risk controller at Switzerland's No. 4 bank, Zuercher Kantonalbank, notes that under pressure to improve returns, banks need to allocate resources to businesses with the best return/risk ratios. ALM, he says, is an area where management needs to take a firm stand on how much risk the institution can support and hedge accordingly.

Even the most sophisticated firms are only beginning to address the question of using risk management for firmwide financial optimization. Andrew Lapkin, vice president with the Bankers Trust Raroc Group, remarks that an understanding of how different aspects of risk management fit together is still lacking. He notes, however, that at the trader-level optimization is more fine-tuned.

Notwithstanding, optimization plays an important role. Any problem at the transaction or portfolio level can be cast in the framework of mathematical optimization. Optimizers are used to manage portfolios over single and multiple periods as well as to execute optimal hedging. The growing role of the mathematics of optimization was noted by many interviewees. Ron Dembo, former Yale University professor and founder of Algorithmics, believes that optimization will become the overarching paradigm of finance in the near future.

1.3 RISK MANAGEMENT AND FINANCIAL INNOVATION

In the 1920s, the Austro-American economist Joseph Schumpeter noted that competitive markets require innovation. In its absence, margins and profits deteriorate. Finance is no exception. Deregulation has increased the competition in finance and brought with it the need to innovate in products, services, and ways of doing business. But financial markets do not lend themselves easily to innovation as products are quite standardized. In the last four decades, there has been relatively little innovation in financial products and processes if compared to what has happened in the consumer or high-tech sectors.

Risk management methodologies are introducing opportunities for innovation. One such area is in the relationship between banks and their clients. Traditionally, clients have been managed on a one-to-one basis. Competition, with the consequent pressure on profits, is putting a strain on this relationship, in particular at the level of the retail client. But banks are also reassessing their relationship with corporate clients.

Dirk-Emma Baestaens of Generale Bank remarks that the centralization of risk management functions is changing relationship banking as the marginal distribution is being assessed product by product. This will force banks to view business potential differently. Some of our interviewees see this as the end of relationship banking, others as the basis for putting relationship banking on a more transparent footing. In any case, Dr. Baestaens notes that the implementation of such a system — not without its difficulties — will impact a firm's ability to survive.

There is the widespread perception that the relationship of financial firms with their clients must become more open, more objective. There will be more sharing of information, more consulting in financial choices. Clients who do not understand what they are buying will increasingly become a liability, as recent highly publicized cases have illustrated. At the same time, more openness implies stricter rules.

There will also be innovation in the internal structuring of organizations and in the structuring of services. Many foresee a restructuring of the financial industry in a chain of multilayered suppliers and marketers, each highly specialized. A number of firms are increasingly structured as virtual companies, i.e., shells that hold an array of suppliers. Though there are probably limits to this process, there will be specialization due to the complexity of financial products and the need to combine global competitiveness with local presence.

One of the most challenging tasks in financial innovation is creating and completing new financial markets. Risk management methodologies are key to this endeavor. The creation and completion of markets for credit risk and, to some extent, insurance risk are widely considered to be emerging sectors of finance.

Credit risk is still poorly understood conceptually and banks are ill prepared to take a market view. Notwithstanding, academic researchers and model builders are actively working to construct the conceptual and modeling tools needed to tackle the problem. The ultimate goal is to create a large market for credit risk attributes. To achieve this, new financial engineering capabilities are required. A number of financial institutions are committed to making this happen.

The drive to productize insurance risk is related to the need to add liquidity to the market. Though there are conceptual problems, insurance and finance can be given a somewhat unified treatment. Insurance can benefit from a financial approach to information handling and finance from an actuarial approach to pricing.

Colin Lawrence, head of global market risk at BZW Barclays in London, believes that the management of credit risk will change banks considerably. "The old-fashioned way of buying and selling units of credit risk was buying or merging with another bank," he says. "The new way is through credit swaps." Dr. Lawrence foresees the possibility of a central agency selecting optimal portfolios for swapping or creating derivatives and, perhaps, risk auditors for evaluation for swap deals. He anticipates an explosion of research in credit risk where, he believes, superior analytics and the ability to crunch numbers will determine who survives in an increasingly oligopolistic market.

Loan portfolio insurance techniques have been in use for a long time. But Generale Bank's Dirk-Emma Baestaens remarks that more than portfolio insurance is needed to manage credit risk. Portfolios, he says, are too small to allow for default substitution. Generale Bank counts among its clients 30,000 small-to-medium-sized firms in Belgium and all big ones, virtually all of the country's companies. Dr. Baestaens cites the need to be able to engineer capital structure swaps between, for example, junior and senior partners or lending types. He foresees the use of specialized credit derivatives as banks move from hedging to optimization, and believes that within the next five years turning credit risk into derivatives will be an important phenomenon.

Innovation in credit risk management has lagged behind that in market risk management. David Townsend, deputy director of Barclays' portfolio management unit attributes this relative delay to a lack of confidence in the technology and the huge cultural shift required. Used to making yes/no decisions, credit managers need to become comfortable in assigning probabilities and pricing loans.

Drawing a parallel with the market for collateralized mortgage obligations (CMOs), Dr. Baestaens adds that the lack of standardization has been holding back innovation. J.P. Morgan's announcement of CreditMetrics may be an important step in the direction of establishing standards. Co-sponsored by major American and European banks and KMV Corporation, the software firm that created the analytics, CreditMetrics provides a sophisticated framework for measuring credit risk that should appeal to major banks.

Some of our interviewees, however, expressed the need for prudence in developing markets for credit and insurance risk. For Jean-Marc Eber of Société Générale's capital markets division in Paris, the market for these products might be inherently incomplete. He sees a number of problems from the theoretical point of view and cautions that opening a market in an incomplete system of markets may leave everyone worse off.

References

Bernstein, Peter L., *Against the Gods: The Remarkable Story of Risk*, John Wiley & Sons, New York, NY, 1996.

Epstein, Larry G. and Tan Wang, "Intertemporal Asset Pricing Under Knightian Uncertainty," *Econometrica*, 62, 283-322, 1994.

Chapter 2

The Theoretical Underpinnings of Risk Management

2.1 TOWARDS A THEORY OF RISK

Risk management lacks an all-encompassing theory that would provide a global description of uncertainties present in the economy and comprehensive tools for modifying those uncertainties. In lieu of a global description, local ad hoc methodologies are fitted to scarce data. But is academic research on theory of interest to the industry? "Yes," says Peter Zangari, vice president of risk management research at J.P. Morgan. "Theory and more academic questions will be of increasing importance as we try to develop a more accurate model of the real world." A model such as RiskMetrics, he notes, is based on a purely statistical approach.

The theoretical underpinnings of risk management must take into account three orders of phenomena: (1) the uncertainties present in the economy, (2) how financial markets react to external uncertainties, and (3) how uncertainties can be modified and/or reduced. An understanding of the practice of risk management implies an understanding of the interplay between external risk and its processing by the financial markets as well as the engineering of hedging strategies.

Technology provides the means, albeit imperfect, of predicting and controlling events. It is responsible for our ability to forecast phenomena such as the weather, reducing our uncertainty about future weather outcomes. But our predictive abilities remain crude. Many events, from environmental catastrophes to social upheavals or the commercial success of an enterprise, cannot be predicted with confidence.

Financial markets allow the trading of contracts that claim the right to future outcomes of economic activity. Prices are based on forecasts of what those outcomes might be. As finance deals with outcomes related to any possible economic activity, including the performance of financial markets themselves, it is not surprising that forecasts are crude.

"Today's finance theory," says Donald van Deventer, president of The Kamakura Corporation, "falls somewhat short of a true description of reality." Such a theory — similar to what exists in the physical sciences — would allow us to predict the future course of events starting from a set of initial data. Instead, we are limited to making rough statistical estimates of the future value of economic variables. Predicting business cycles or even rough business indices with any accuracy still remains beyond our capability.

Given the uncertainty about future events, risk is managed through investment selection and contractual agreements for exchanging risk. The development of risk management methodologies is an endeavor in improving our ability to predict future events. Though the predictive aspect of risk management might not be evident, forecasting is at the core of managing risk. It should be noted, however, that forecasting is not the sure prediction of some event, but the evaluation of probability distributions at some time horizon. Forecasts carry uncertainty, i.e., they entail risk.

The theoretical underpinnings of risk management are, therefore, the structural and statistical regularities present in the economy. The ability to build financial market models provides the probabilistic setting; the rest is pure statistical aggregation.

To illustrate the aggregation properties, in tossing a fair coin, we are totally uncertain as to a heads or tails outcome. If, however, we toss the coin 1000 times, we are certain that we will get close to 50/50 heads and tails. Despite the expectation of regularity, explaining this certainty is difficult. In applying probability concepts to finance, we assume that we have a probabilistic knowledge of a number of economic events backed by statistical measurement. Because there are regularities that are stable in time, we also assume that the past can somehow predict the future.

Probabilities can be engineered, limiting the scope of uncertainty of selected events. By diversifying portfolios, we reduce uncertainty. Anticorrelated risks can be aggregated, stabilizing outcomes. Once we have accepted a probabilistic knowledge of the economy combined with market laws, we have the means to reduce uncertainty by aggregating probabilities. By writing appropriate contracts, e.g. options or swaps, we increase our ability to engineer events with desired probabilities.

2.2 FINANCE THEORY AS THE FRAMEWORK FOR RISK MANAGEMENT

The theoretical framework for risk management is provided primarily by finance theory. Finance theory, however, provides only the modeling of how financial markets work. As risk management evolves from a control function to a financial optimization function, the role of both economic theory and data analysis grows. Economic theory and data analysis allow, in fact, to identify and forecast risk factors. We will therefore explore the relationship between finance theory, factor analysis, and the forecasting of factors.

At the core of finance theory is the representation and measurement of uncertainty on the evolution of economic variables. These quantities include primarily prices, dividends, interest rates, currency rates, but might also encompass economic parameters such as GNP or unemployment indicators. The mathematical representation of the uncertain evolution of financial quantities is based on the notion of "states" of the economy. A state of the economy can be identified with a complete possible path of all economic variables.

It is our lack of knowledge of the current state of the economy (i.e., the path that the economy follows over the entire period) that produces uncertainty. Consider a period of time from 0 to T and all the possible histories of the economy over that period, i.e., all the possible paths of the set of economic variables. We might take a discrete-time view in which case only discrete points in time are considered, or a continuous-time view in which case paths will be defined over the entire interval $[0, T]$.

The notion of uncertainty is dynamic: information is revealed through time. At the beginning of a period, there is complete uncertainty as regards the path that the economy is following. With the passing of time, information is revealed and the set of possible paths is constrained to those paths whose initial section coincides with what actually happened. At the end of the period, there is certainty as the entire path is revealed.

Uncertainty is quantified by assuming that probabilities can be assigned to events, i.e., sets of possible paths. At the beginning of the period, the probability assignments of the entire space of possible paths have to be considered. As time passes and information is revealed, the space on which probabilities have to be evaluated is progressively restricted. The probabilities themselves are conditional probabilities given the information revealed up to that point.

The stochastic representation of the economy can be schematized as in Figure 2.1. The outer circle represents the set Ω of possible states. Each state $\omega \in \Omega$ is identified with the complete history of economic variables X over the period $[0,T]$. Probabilities are assigned to sets of states, that is to say, to events such as A or B.

Figure 2.1

The economy is represented as a probability space of states; each state is a complete history of the economy.

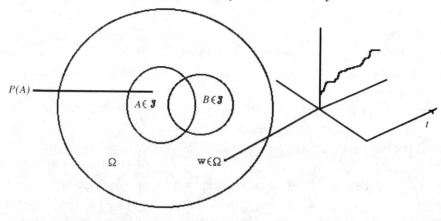

This, rather informally expressed, is the mathematical foundation of finance theory. It might seem counter-intuitive; thinking in terms of instantaneous states of the economy might seem more natural. One could effectively adopt the point of view of instantaneous states, but this would require the construction of a global space to link probabilities over different times. It is logically easier to assume upfront a probability space made up of all the possible economic histories. For the formal mathematical definition of the concepts used for the stochastic description of the economy, see Appendix A.2.1.

Given this global description of the economy, finance theory imposes a number of constraints on processes. These constraints act as the "laws of motion" of the system. Constraints are of two types: those that do not assume any description of agents and those that depend on such a description. The former, embodied by the no-arbitrage principle, are by far the most important in risk management. The latter, the constraints of equilibrium and optimality, are of limited practical use.

In determining constraints, finance theory needs to solve the problem of the self-referentiality of markets. This quality refers to the fact that financial markets react to external events as well as to their own expectations. Modeling self-referentiality is difficult and present finance theory does not attempt it.

To avoid this difficulty, the conceptual shortcut is to: (1) assume that markets reach their decisions through some unspecified mechanism and (2) observe what implications can be drawn about the time evolution of financial quantities. This is key. Finance theory does not determine the *causal* link between present conditions and the ensuing market reaction. Rather it looks at the end products, i.e., dividend-price processes, to determine if these have any special properties that could be expressed as mathematical constraints. To render the problem mathematically tractable, the idealization of perfect complete markets is made.

Assumed to be too small individually to influence the market, economic agents are considered to be price-takers. Price processes, however, must be coherent with their collective action. It is assumed that agents are competent and fully informed and that they exploit any profit opportunity present in the market, thus realigning prices. This is the notion of efficient markets. The most fundamental expression of market efficiency is the absence of the possibility of making unbounded profits, i.e., the no-arbitrage principle.

The no-arbitrage constraint states that it is not possible to make a sure gain with no initial investment. Though the essence is simple, the precise statement of the no-arbitrage principle is complex; it is a mathematical condition that can be stated for any set of stochastic processes, regardless of what they represent.

The no-arbitrage principle is a global condition that links all processes over the entire period of time under consideration. It is not sufficient in and of itself to determine the price dynamics of all securities; it can only determine a set of security prices given another set of security prices. If, for instance, a trading strategy replicates the dividend process of some security, the no-arbitrage principle determines the price of that security. This is the basis of option theory. In linking all prices, it provides a coherent framework for risk management.

Important as theoretical concepts, agent optimality and equilibrium assume an idealized description of agents. The description is, however, difficult to represent explicitly. In practice, agents are described by utility functions defined over the entire stochastic processes of securities. It is then assumed that agents optimize their utility functions. Equilibrium is reached if every agent can independently maximize his or her own utility function, remaining compatible with other agents.

Agent optimality does not address the question of how agents effectively process available information. Quite the contrary, it remains an abstract descripion of markets. Clearly an idealization, agent optimality is of little practical use.

By imposing the no-arbitrage constraint, some processes are made to depend on others, e.g., derivatives processes depend on the underlyings. What is left out are some fundamental processes that we assume as risk determinants. The entire time evolution of these basic risk determinants has to be described. In the physical sciences, we are generally able to derive the future evolution of a system from a set of initial and boundary conditions of the same system. In finance theory, on the other hand, we have to specify the entire time evolution of some part of the system in order to describe the evolution of the rest of the system. Figure 2.2 illustrates these aspects of the difference between the physical sciences and option theory.

Figure 2.2

Finance theory is not an input/output theory. The laws of physics (upper graph) allow to compute the future evolution of a system starting from a set of initial conditions of the same system. In finance, however, option theory (lower graph) requires the specification of basic processes over the entire period (thick line); derived processes (thin line) can then be computed.

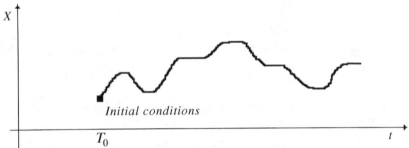

The paradigm of physics: initial conditions determine the evolution of the system.

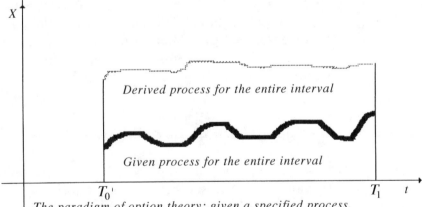

The paradigm of option theory: given a specified process, derived processes are determined.

Risk determinants are subject to additional constraints that depend on deeper economic forces than the price adjustment process of financial markets. Presently, however, there is no economic theory characterized by a level of mathematical sophistication comparable to that of the option theory. As a consequence, it is statistical analysis and data-mining algorithms more than economic theory that impose economic constraints.

The major components in risk management theory can be summarized as follows:

- stochastic processes for modeling risk determinants, i.e., models of uncertainty that are fitted to data through statistical estimates and/or adaptive methods;
- theoretical constraints that can be imposed on sets of individual models. The key constraint is the no-arbitrage principle;
- economic constraints on the factors, generally provided by data analysis.

Present theories on the functioning of financial markets suffer from a major shortcoming: they are not an input/output theory such as physics; we cannot identify initial external risk factors and observe how financial markets react to them. Instead, the need is for independent forecasts that the theory, in its most accomplished form, cannot provide. Present theories are, nevertheless, widely accepted. This acceptance is coupled with the belief that there is no theoretical breakthrough in sight. There are, however, new and promising areas of research and development in economic modeling; Chapter 7 explores some of these.

2.3 THE ASSUMPTION OF PERFECT MARKETS

Finance theory makes a number of simplifying hypotheses on the functioning of financial markets. These are summarized in the assumption of perfect competitive markets. Clearly an idealization, this assumption consists of three basic postulates:

- markets are characterized by the absence of friction and default, and there are neither transaction costs nor impediments to trading;
- agents are price-takers;
- there are no arbitrage opportunities.

Commenting on present finance theory, Robert Jarrow, Ronald P. and Susan E. Lynch professor of investment management at Cornell University's Johnson Graduate School of Management and co-developer of the Heath-Jarrow-Morton interest rate model, remarks that science consists in identifying a set of postulates and deriving implications from them. If postulates have reasonable consequences, i.e., consequences that fit empirical data with reasonable precision, they are accepted. Often there are competing sets of postulates that explain experimental data with different levels of accuracy.

The postulates accepted in the physical sciences have implications that benefit from a high degree of empirical verification; the postulates of finance theory do not benefit from such a high degree of verification. In looking at the postulates of current finance theory, in particular the hypotheses related to perfect competitive markets, Prof. Jarrow explores their robustness and analyzes if and how they can be relaxed without a major revision of the theory.

A number of today's hypotheses, Prof. Jarrow notes, can effectively be relaxed. The hypothesis of frictionless markets is an idealization that can be relaxed, though at some computational cost. The no-default hypothesis, though reasonably robust, is an idealization that can also be relaxed. (Jarrow and Turnbull, 1995, presented a framework for introducing counterparty risk.) The theory of the evolution of market prices is pretty robust and, though difficult to handle on computers, is handled well conceptually.

Next come the hypotheses of market completeness and no-arbitrage. Market completeness means that any cashflow can be obtained as a result of investing in a trading strategy. If markets are complete, any new security can be replicated by a trading strategy and priced by no-arbitrage arguments. The market completeness hypothesis can be dropped, Prof. Jarrow says, but at the expense of pricing theory. In absence of completeness, the mathematics of pricing becomes complex.

The no-arbitrage hypothesis — the key constraint used in financial modeling — is well tested empirically: despite all the efforts, true arbitrage opportunities have not been found. Prof. Jarrow believes that both the no-arbitrage and the market-completeness hypotheses are more robust than current modeling suggests. In a recent paper (1996), he shows that even phenomena such as bubbles can be consistent with no-arbitrage.

The only assumption of perfect competitive markets that Prof. Jarrow considers critical — one which would change risk management — is the competitive price assumption, i.e., the price-taking assumption. "Relax this hypothesis," he says, "and the whole price structure changes, introducing a new equilibrium with asymmetric information, order flows, and motivation for trading."

2.4 THE NO-ARBITRAGE PRINCIPLE

The no-arbitrage hypothesis is simple in its statement — it is not possible to make a *sure* gain with no initial investment — but somewhat complex in its mathematical formulation. Suppose that security prices are represented by a set of stochastic processes, i.e., random variables indexed by time. A trading strategy is a stochastic process that represents the composition of the portfolios held at every instant. At each trading date, agents trade, changing the composition of their portfolios. In the finite case, a trading strategy is a set of random numbers for each trading date. These numbers represent the proportion of each security held after trading. In continuous time, one has to think in terms of portfolios that change continuously in time.

To state the no-arbitrage principle, the gain of a trading strategy must be defined. This is simple in the finite case where the gain of a trading strategy is the sum of the differences of a portfolio's value for each trading interval. This is also a stochastic process as there is a gain for each state in each instant. If, however, continuous-time trading is admitted, the limits of this process for very short trading intervals must be taken. Taking limits implies the notion of stochastic integral, which requires considerable mathematics to define. (See Appendix A.2.2 for a formal definition of stochastic calculus and A.2.3 for a formal definition of the no-arbitrage principle.)

A trading strategy is called self-financing if the total gain of the strategy is reinvested, i.e., if there is no inflow or outflow of capital. This is simple to understand in the finite case: it means that at every trading date the portfolios held by agents have the same value after trading as before. One might imagine that agents sell their entire portfolio and invest the proceeds in a new portfolio of equal value. The definition of a self-financing trading strategy in the limit of continuous time again requires the notion of stochastic integral. The no-arbitrage hypothesis — which states that there is no self-financing trading strategy that has only non-negative values with positive values in some states — is equivalent to stating that there is no sure gain without any investment. As a consequence, any risk-free investment must earn the same risk-free rate.

If one admits continuous time and/or an infinite time horizon and/or an infinite number of securities in the mathematical representation, there are additional mathematical subtleties in the no-arbitrage concept. There is, for instance, the need to rule out trivial strategies exemplified by doubling at roulette, a strategy which yields a gain with probability one but makes variance unbounded, i.e., it requires infinite capital.

There are two important aspects in the no-arbitrage principle. The first is that it precludes the creation of value from nothing, a seemingly sound economic principle. The second is that eventual arbitrage opportunities would imply some knowledge of the future with certainty as this would imply the knowledge of a self-financing trading strategy that yields no losses with probability one. In finance theory, information and gains are closely related. As sure unbounded gains are not likely in the real economy, the no-arbitrage principle imposes that whenever there is certainty no sure gain can be made.

Most financial models are based on some variation of the no-arbitrage principle. Thomas Ho, co-developer of the Ho-Lee interest-rate model and president of the consulting and software firm GAT, remarks that the application of arbitrage-free conditions can be extended to all equity options. This includes optionality that derives from factors such as prepayment behavior. GAT's model integrates the market and behavioral phenomena such as depositor behavior in retail banking or lapsed policies in the insurance industry.

From a practical standpoint, questions involving the no-arbitrage principle are due to the fact that the no-arbitrage condition applies to models that are only approximate. Approximation means that models do not fit data perfectly and need to be calibrated. In some cases, the calibration of models reveals discrepancies that can be viewed as arbitrage opportunities.

In fact, traders often try to find arbitrage opportunities. They might do so by comparing actual data with reference data from models. There might be discrepancies between, for instance, the computed term structure of interest rates and actual data. Traders interpret these discrepancies as arbitrage opportunities and try to exploit them. What they really find, however, are not arbitrage opportunities but situations that might lead to a high profit with a high probability. Figure 2.3 illustrates how, using different models that fit market data only approximately, traders might interpret the discrepancies between computed values and empirical data as arbitrage opportunities.

Figure 2.3

Financial models fit market data only approximately. Calibrating models to fit data might reveal discrepancies that can be perceived as arbitrage opportunities.

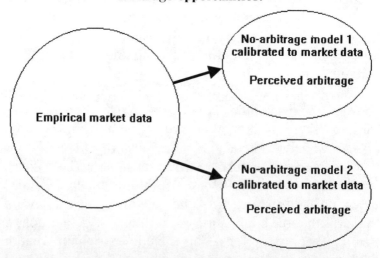

The problem, says Yu Zhu, director of risk assessment and control at Sakura Global Capital in New York, is one of how to handle approximations. New theoretical direction is being given by market models, but their implementation is tricky. The most important aspect for practitioners, Dr. Zhu says, is to calibrate to market information; if not, traders see arbitrage opportunities and do not trust the model. "But," he adds, "if you must calibrate, can you still maintain arbitrage-free?"

Farshid Jamshidian (1996), head of product development and strategic trading at Sakura Global Capital in London, developed a theory of market models of the term structure of interest rates. The model takes as the basic market data Libor and swap rates and volatilities instead of the usual bond yields. It has the advantage of automatically calibrating to market prices of either caps or swaptions in a manner consistent with the widely used Black-Scholes model. However, Dr. Jamshidian demonstrated that it is not possible to achieve this simultaneously for Libor and swap rates; the Black-Scholes model for caps and swaption are simply not consistent. Dr. Jamshidian's conclusion: while such model inconsistency may imply an arbitrage opportunity in theory, it is not of a magnitude that can be exploited in practice. "The important thing," Dr. Jamshidian says, "is that the model is well adapted to the products under question and captures their peculiar hedging difficulties."

2.5 FACTOR ANALYSIS AND ECONOMIC CONSTRAINTS

The no-arbitrage constraint allows to express some quantity in function of others, for instance derivatives prices in function of the underlying. Given a portfolio of stocks and options, some general model is assumed for the underlying stocks, say an Ito process, and options are modeled through the no-arbitrage constraint. The latter is a financial constraint, due to the functioning of markets.

A number of financial quantities remain, however, as the basic stochastic processes, i.e., as the key risk factors of models. The no-arbitrage principle might leave undecided a large number of risk determinants, thus generating complex models. In a one-period model, for instance, there may be hundreds of key rates and, therefore, a large variance-covariance matrix.

In general, these risk determinants will be subject to other constraints, due not to the functioning of markets but to the structural features of the economy. These additional constraints would reduce risk factors to a number of fundamental risk determinants, i.e., a number of basic economic variables that determine the evolution of the entire market.

Future improvements in our ability to manage risk depend on our ability to improve our understanding of risk determinants. This, in turn, depends on improved data analysis capabilities and, ultimately, on our theoretical understanding of the economy.

This point was made by Chi-fu Huang, formerly J.C. Penney professor of finance at MIT and now a principal of Long-Term Capital Management. Dr. Huang remarks that there are basically two theoretical approaches to risk management. The first, the mean-variance theory, is the easiest to implement and is widely used on Wall Street. The mean-variance approach requires attention to specific issues, such as how to capture rare events and what kind of probabilities are entailed by fat-tail distributions. Generating the parameters for rare events without the lifetime data remains, says Dr. Huang, "pure art." He notes two deficiencies with the mean-variance approach: (1) people make decisions in a dynamic fashion and (2) the approach may not capture true risk determinants as many cofactors are missing.

The second theoretical approach to risk management, Dr. Huang remarks, is through factor analysis. This requires the identification of macroeconomic factors and their projection onto the relevant economic variables. The difficulty here lies in selecting the important economic variables.

This step would require theoretical knowledge — at this stage limited — to add constraints of an economic nature in addition to the purely financial no-arbitrage principle. In fact, understanding these constraints means understanding the functioning of the economy, identifying the key variables and the links between them and other variables. The result of the process is a reduced set of risk determinants (see Figure 2.4).

Figure 2.4
The cascading of financial constraints (i.e., no arbitrage) plus economic constraints results in a reduced set of risk determinants.

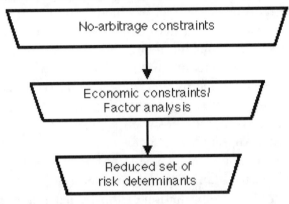

In its generality, identifying factors is the problem of science; science is the quest for the most parsimonious explanation of phenomena. That goal has been achieved to an amazing degree in the physical sciences. In economics, understanding factors means understanding, in scientific quantitative terms, the dynamics of the economy.

Factor analysis can be performed at various levels, using theoretical knowledge to identify factors or as a mathematical factorization method. For an introduction to the methodologies of factor analysis, see Appendix A.2.4.

2.6 THE THEORETICAL FRAMEWORK FOR FORECASTING

It is often said that forecasting entails the assumption that the future will repeat the past. In a sense, this statement is obvious: it is the enabling condition of science. We do not expect that tomorrow's physical laws will be different from today's. The precise statement of just what laws are constant over time is what science is all about. This might be difficult or elusive to establish for financial markets and economic systems. Simplifications and approximations are in order.

The simplest forecasting method is unconditional forecasting, which considers a time series as an unstructured set of data whose statistical distribution has to be estimated. Some risk management systems make this assumption explicitly and use more or less sophisticated schemes for deciding the lookback period. Better forecasting performance can be obtained through conditional forecasting, which makes forecasts of events at a certain moment conditional to events at previous moments.

Conditional forecasting assumes that the successive points of a time series are generated by a *data generation process* (DGP) i.e., it assumes that there are recognizable (but not necessarily constant) mathematical relationships between successive points in a set of time series. (See Appendix A.2.5 for an introduction to the mathematical theory of forecasting.) The simplest forecasting hypothesis is linearity. Linearity implies that the value of a time series at a certain instant is a linear combination of the values at a number of previous points plus error terms. Statistical methods such as the Box-Jenkins method prescribe how to fit linear parameters.

Conditional forecasting methodologies can be extended to cover the nonlinear case. The use of neural networks as forecasting devices is based on the assumption that there is a stable nonlinear relationship between successive points in a time series. Learning methodologies such as backpropagation are used to best approximate this relationship with a set of predetermined functions that depend on the type and topology of the network.

These schemes typically "learn" from secondary variables obtained through the preprocessing of raw data. An advantage of secondary variables is that they allow the consideration of more general relationships. For instance, by taking difference ratios as secondary variables, differential equations can be approximated.

Adaptive methodologies such as neural networks are ad hoc methodologies whose application has to be evaluated case by case. There is no generalized theory that prescribes the shape of forecasting relationships. Chaos theory has provided some unifying concepts but falls short of being a generalized theory of financial forecasting. Nonetheless, it is interesting to note a number of generalized empirical findings about forecasting financial series. These statistical findings, referred to as stylized facts, include heteroschedasticity and scaling laws.

Heteroschedasticity is essentially the clustering of volatilities. In simple terms, it refers to the fact that periods of sustained high volatility are followed by periods of sustained low volatility. The precise statement of heteroschedasticity is embodied in the X-ARCH family of models which includes the ARCH and GARCH models. A well established empirical finding, heteroschedasticity has not yet been explained by theory. Explanations based on the aggregation of agents' decisions have been advanced (see Lux, 1996, and Aoki, 1996); these factors signal a change in macroeconomic explanations.

From the practical point of view, the X-ARCH models have been useful: they model explicitly the time variation of risk variants. Their value has been not so much in making point forecasts of volatility as in modeling volatility over relatively long periods of time. This allows X-ARCH models to be successfully combined with other financial modeling.

Olsen & Associates, a Zurich-based developer of financial software, applied their proprietary deseasonalization technology together with the HARCH process to capture the volatility clustering and fat-tailed distribution of financial time series. According to Rakhal Davé, head of risk management research at Olsen & Associates, a stochastic process such as HARCH fit over 30 minutes and allowed to repeatedly run over 48 intervals per day can produce a better conditional distribution over the one-day horizon than a conditional Gaussian process fit over one day. Dr. Davé believes that the high-frequency data approach has the advantage of making the fit more robust as there are more non-overlapping 30-minute intervals available for fitting the process than one-day intervals.

Scaling laws — the other important set of empirical findings on financial time series — state that similar patterns are found at different coarse grainings of time. First discovered by Benoit Mandelbrot in cotton price series, scaling laws have been successively found in many financial time series. In studying the USD-DM exchange rate over the period February 1986-September 1993, U. A. Mueller et al (1993) at Olsen & Associates found scaling laws of absolute price changes in the currencies (see Figure 2.5). Though the implications are not yet fully understood, scaling laws seem to allow the use of a large body of well known mathematical results on scaling and perturbation.

Figure 2.5

Scaling law of absolute price changes.

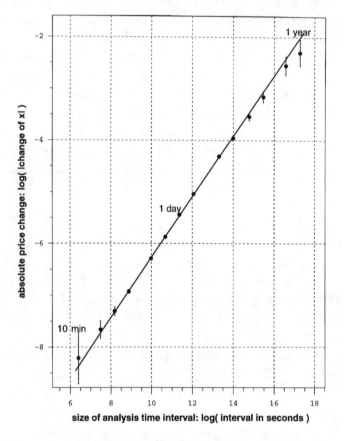

FX rate: USD-DEM; sampling period: from February 1986 to September 1993. Double-logarithmic plot. The vertical bars indicate the standard errors of the observations. (Courtesy of Olsen & Associates)

In summary, there is yet no generalized theory for forecasting which would amount to a causal theory of economics. There are ad hoc methodologies based on the assumption of the existence of stable patterns in financial time series. There are a number of empirical generalized findings, namely heteroschedasticity and scaling laws. A more comprehensive use of concepts from statistical mechanics might prove useful in this endeavor.

2.7 DATA MINING

Thomas Ho, co-developer of the Ho-Lee interest-rate model and president of GAT, notes that option pricing theory has made tremendous progress in the last 10 years, going from arbitrage-free pricing to managing the whole trading flow in a consistent framework. But, he adds, it is not yet possible to roll risk sources up to the firm level. To do so, Dr. Ho believes, would require an arbitrage-free framework plus a theory of risk management.

While the no-arbitrage principle is the law of the market that binds the behavior of different securities, it is not sufficient for managing risk; an understanding of the fundamental risk determinants is required. Risk management models include, by necessity, a representation of the basic risk determinants. Given our present scientific understanding of the economy, identifying what factors are determinant and how they impact other factors is a question of data mining and statistical estimates, eventually complemented by macroeconomic modeling.

Among our interviewees, data analysis is widely considered the key problem in risk measurement. Many might still find risk management analytics difficult as they involve complex mathematics. It seems clear, however, that the truly challenging task is determining the sources of risk and their correlations where no tenable theory might be invoked.

Michael Winchell, senior managing director in charge of risk management at Bear Stearns, comments on the importance of data. He notes that a lot of time is spent discussing the advantages and limitations of various mathematical methods or whether to use Monte Carlo simulation or binomial trees, when too little effort is expended on data collection and the accurate representation of positions and transactions.

At Morgan Stanley, Harry Mendell, vice president in the market risk department, notes that the biggest problem in modeling is extracting data from the database in such a way as to get an accurate reading. "If the data is not sliced and mapped properly to the correct risk factors," he says, "all the modeling in the world won't help." Mr. Mendell suggests sitting down with the trader and interviewing him, asking questions like "What bet are you putting on?" The key, he says, is understanding risk factors and he cautions on the assumptions made in importing data. "A gold-desk trader," Mr. Mendell remarks, "might ultimately be an interest-rate trader."

New data-mining methodologies might help in understanding risk factors. Data mining has made tremendous progress in the last ten years thanks to the availability of computing power and transaction data. Among the new methodologies are techniques that segment markets into maximally homogeneous partitions. When applied to risk management, these techniques help in grouping together securities or clients that are similar. Appendix A.2.6 provides a resume of data-mining techniques, including supervised and unsupervised learning schemes.

Factor analysis itself has made progress. In addition to standard statistical techniques, new adaptive methods can be used. Among them Kohonen maps and other neural-network based techniques offer the ability to capture a high level of nonlinearity in factorization.

Data mining is useful in other areas as well. Virtually every model depends on market calibration and on the specification of some parameter. Specifying parameters is a question of statistical estimates and data mining. Option prices, for instance, depend on the volatility of the underlying stock if one uses a constant volatility model. To determine option prices, it is therefore necessary to estimate volatilities. Estimates imply data.

Chi-fu Huang, formerly professor of finance at MIT and now a principal at Long-Term Capital Management, remarks that data are also needed to select models. "Data and the model," Dr. Huang comments, "are two sides of a coin." But as all models are mis-specified, the most that can be said is that model A is better than model B for purpose X. Dr. Huang cites the need of a loss function for the purpose one wants to achieve by using models and a set of tools for making statistical inferences.

The technique of statistical estimates is rather complex; processes are not stationary and probabilities change over time. This is the major difficulty in applying probability concepts to finance. One cannot invoke stationarity and confidently exchange expected values with time statistics. From the standpoint of estimates, it's necessary to understand how far back in time it's possible to go.

For Victor Makarov, vice president of Chase's Client Risk Management Services, "the key is to determine the lookback period: how much data do you take?" Dr. Makarov observes that the amount of data required is a compromise between the statistical requirement for large samples and structural changes in the economy which constrain the size of the data sample. In fact, in taking samples, data should not overlap periods in which markets experienced structural change.

Dr. Makarov adds that volatility determines the lookback period. The more stable the time series, the longer the interval taken; in absence of stability, he suggests taking the current cluster. In practice, if the goal is to look forward one day, Dr. Makarov suggests a 50 to 200-day lookback period, using backtesting to determine the amount of data to use. "But," he cautions, "if intervals are constantly being changed, numbers are no longer consistent."

There are other issues related to estimating parameters. One is the use of market data to predict other data. Traders, for instance, often use implied volatility to forecast actual volatility. In other words, the market consensus on prices is translated into volatilities, applying standard models. This is a procedure similar to that of finding arbitrage opportunities referred to previously.

Dr. Makarov notes that there are two sources of volatility information, implied volatility and historical data. It would be tempting, he says, to use implied volatility for risk management as, in doing so, one would use the same parameters for both pricing and risk management. Unfortunately, Dr. Makarov adds, it doesn't work: there are not sufficiently developed markets that include options on all positions and all combinations of positions, possible strikes, and all maturities and instruments. He suggests a non-parametric approach in time-series analysis, avoiding statements on normal/abnormal distributions.

2.8 MACROECONOMIC MODELING

An understanding of the fundamental risk determinants is of growing importance as the objective of risk management shifts from a control function to one of financial optimization. Presently, our primary sources for understanding risk determinants are statistics and data-mining methodologies. Macroeconomics, however, also plays a role. This role is destined to grow as macroeconomics arrives at a more faithful description of empirical data.

Macroeconomics provides a theoretical understanding of the evolution of the underlying economic quantities and, therefore, of the forces ultimately driving financial markets. In its classical formulation, it deals with broad aggregates of economic quantities. Macroeconomic variables include quantities such as GNP or the monetary mass, and parameters such as inflation and interest rates. Models are sets of equations that link these parameters, providing insight on co-movements of macro aggregates.

A major tenet of present macroeconomics is the rational expectations hypothesis. According to the latter, as usually stated, forecasted processes are the same as actual processes. This formulation requires qualification. Stated more precisely, the rational expectations hypothesis means that actual processes are equilibrium processes. The validity of today's macroeconomic theory is being questioned; Chapter 7 presents a summary of criticisms and a survey of new avenues of research in macroeconomic modeling.

The theoretical formulation of macroeconomics does not exhibit a specific, validated functional relationship between variables, i.e., an economic "world utility function" that could be used in computations. Macroeconomics posits that macroeconomic variables are linked by a set of functions but, generally speaking, the actual form of these functions remains unspecified. A major effort is under way to understand what links need to be posited and to develop the analytical consequences of these hypotheses given unspecified functional dependencies.

To perform calculations, econometrics makes simplifying hypotheses on functional relationships. These hypotheses are typically embodied in linear approximations that include free parameters. The latter are estimated using well known statistical techniques. Clearly an approximation, econometrics has the advantage of practical applicability. However, the need to make linear approximations often imposes the use of large sets of variables.

Macroeconomic modeling can be useful in many risk management contexts. In credit risk management, these models are used to regress failure rates over relevant macroeconomic variables, offering insight into corporate failures. Macroeconomic models are used in stock portfolio management, to forecast those factors that explain the evolution of stock prices. They are also important, remarks Yong Li, risk manager at Credit Lyonnais Americas, in creating event-based scenarios, linking the scenarios to key yield curves as inflation and GNP. Mr. Li, who is also director of risk management education at GARP (Global Association of Risk Professionals), believes that the integration of skills in financial analytics and macroeconomic modeling will play a growing role as market and credit risk management converge.

2.9 THE TERM STRUCTURE OF INTEREST RATES

Interest rates are a fundamental risk determinant. They are of special importance to fixed-income portfolios whose value is determined essentially by a combination of interest rates and credit risk. They are also important to banks whose lending-borrowing spreads they can seriously affect.

Interest rates are represented not by a single number but by an entire curve. In fact, at any moment there are risk-free securities, typically government bonds, that imply an interest rate for each of their maturities. There are at least as many interest rates as there are different maturities. Assuming that there are risk-free bonds that mature at every future instant, there is a continuous yield curve. This curve provides a representation of the term structure of interest rates.

A first practical problem is to determine a mathematical expression for the current term structure given that, in practice, there are only a finite number of maturities of actual bonds. This is a problem of fitting a curve to a number of points, i.e., of calibrating the term-structure curve to current market data. It is not a trivial problem: each best-fit criterion has financial implications.

Uncertainty about interest rates is given by the time evolution of the term structure. With the passing of time, this curve can experience parallel shifts; it might also change shape. An important modeling question is, therefore, how to represent the evolution of the term structure coherent with market data.

There are many interest-rate models. Each makes some assumption as regards the processes that are taken as a given. The initial framework assumed short-term interest rates as a given and modeled them through geometric Brownian motion as if they were stocks. This is not realistic: geometric Brownian motion diverges with the passing of time; interest rates remain confined in some band.

More realistic single-factor models have been proposed. These include a mean-reversion term that pulls interest rates back to some long-term average. Because these models depend on only one Brownian motion, they require the specification of only one uncertainty factor. It is possible to build multifactor models. Once the short-rate process is modeled, the term structure can be modeled in consequence.

An important question is how well models fit the present term structure as empirically observed through the price of bonds of different maturities. Single-factor models need to be approximately calibrated to market data. Other models, however, assume as a given an arbitrage-free system of bond prices. Called arbitrage-free interest-rate models, they fit exactly the present term structure.

At Cornell University, David Heath, Robert Jarrow and Andrew Morton, now with Lehman Brothers, proposed a general methodology — the Heath-Jarrow-Morton (HJM) model — for deriving interest-rate models that agree with an arbitrage-free system of bond prices. The HJM methodology is very general and can be extended to any number of risk factors. It generates models that fit exactly the present term structure. It is, however, demanding in terms of computational resources.

Farshid Jamshidian (1996) built on earlier work by Marek Musiela (University of New South Wales), and developed a theory of interest rates based on forward Libor and swap rate measures and volatilities. Models based on this theory are called market models. They allow a better fitting of the term structure to empirically measurable initial parameters. For the mathematical formulation of various models of the term structure of interest rates, see Appendix A.2.7.

The importance of term-structure interest-rate models to risk management is underlined by Chi-fu Huang. They are, he says a "key element" in risk management. They prescribe the variation in the value of fixed-income portfolios and their derivatives. They also prescribe the evolution of any interest-rate derivative.

Thomas Daula, a managing director in global risk management at Bankers Trust, remarks that while a lot of attention has been focused on term-structure models that replicate current prices of interest-rate derivative products, it is perhaps time to shift emphasis to examine how well the models predict the evolution of prices through time.

These remarks reiterate the growing importance of forecasting in risk management. While a primary concern of the derivatives business is the coherence of an arbitrage-free system of prices, risk management shows a growing concern for the forecasting of risk determinants such as interest rates.

2.10 PRICING RISK

Risk management requires a proper understanding of the value attached to risk. Decisions about risk-return trade-offs imply the measurement of risk premia. There are two complementary questions as regards the price of risk. The first is how financial markets price risk; the second is how agents price risk in the absence of a market mechanism. Before exploring these questions, however, let's look at how risk premia are represented in finance theory.

Intuitively, risk being an objective feature of the economy, risk-averse investors compensate for it by requiring a higher return from or, equivalently, attaching a lower price to risky investments. However, the assumption of investors' risk-aversion is not easy to quantify. In fact, risk aversion is embodied in the shape of utility functions. Unless simplifications are made, the relationship between risk aversion and price processes is a complex one.

The representation of the pricing of risk depends on the representation of the stochastic processes adopted. Most mathematical descriptions of dividend-price processes adopted in finance theory, from linear multifactor models to Ito processes, include two variable coefficients: the (instantaneous) expected return and the (instantaneous) volatility. Given a process of this type, the quantity usually referred to as the *market price of risk* is the difference between the instantaneous expected return and the risk-free rate divided by the instantaneous volatility. In a rather loose sense, the market price of risk represents the return premium for bearing units of risk, i.e., volatility.

In a number of cases, the notion of the market price of risk as defined above cannot be applied. Discontinuous jump processes, for example, cannot be characterized by instantaneous return and volatility: these would be either zero or infinite. Nor can point processes such as Poisson processes be characterized with instantaneous returns and volatilities. Still, these and many other processes are used to describe events such as corporate default. However because of the wide use of continuous-time Ito processes, the market price of risk is a well known representation.

Given the market price of risk for a complete set of independent risk factors, the return and volatility, and thus the market price of risk, of any other derivative security is determined by no-arbitrage arguments. If processes are described through Ito processes, i.e., through instantaneous return and volatility, no-arbitrage arguments constrain these parameters for any redundant process, i.e., for any process that can be replicated through a trading strategy. If securities are described by other types of processes, such as jump processes, the no-arbitrage principle still applies, but the actual representation of the pricing depends on the specific mathematical form of processes.

While the no-arbitrage principle constrains redundant processes, the market price of risk of independent factors remains arbitrary. One factor might command a higher risk premium than another. This might be due, for instance, to the fact that some factors affect strategic markets for which there is a high demand. Ultimately, the value attached to risk depends on the interplay between demand and supply. Contrary to what might seem intuitive, neither the no-arbitrage principle nor the risk aversion of agents imposes that higher volatility be correlated to higher expected returns.

Given a set of dividend-price processes and a trading strategy, it is possible to compute any other measure of risk, for instance VaR. This computation might be onerous as it relies on simulation. The link between measures such as VaR and the return of a trading strategy might be complex or even inconclusive in terms of establishing a risk pricing relationship.

One might ask if there is any theory that explains the pricing of risk. Does the market implement any long-term equilibrium pricing of risk? Within the present framework of finance theory, the attitude towards risk is a given represented by the utility function of agents; the pricing of risk factors is not explained theoretically.

Theories that link, quantitatively, the risk aversion of agents to parameters such as wealth through notions of long-term statistical equilibrium are only now beginning to appear. These theories imply a conceptual shift towards notions of the statistical equilibrium of aggregates of agents. There are complex relationships that link risk premia to the behavioral parameters of agents. A much better insight into the functioning of markets is needed to understand how gains are attributed to different risk behavior.

If there is a market, it is the market as a collective decision-making process that sets the price of risk. In a number of cases, however, firms have to make independent risk pricing decisions: insurance firms set premia and banks price loans even if these contracts are not traded securities. In these cases, a *rational* way of pricing risk, taking into account the time evolution of risky investments, is required.

The insurance industry provides criteria for pricing risk: the actuarial criteria for risk pricing. Actuarial models link premia to the probability of ruin given stochastic processes that describe the occurrence of adverse events; actuarial criteria optimize the repartition of premia among different risk classes.

But even in the absence of a market for trading contracts, financial and insurance firms are subject to market laws. The market is not monopolistic. Prices must be set high enough to be remunerative, but competitive enough to attract clients. As insurance and banking products such as loans begin to be traded in financial markets, a cross fertilization of ideas and methodologies is occurring.

2.11 SIMULATION AND STRESS ANALYSIS

Risk measurement is a multidimensional process. Because data are not sufficient to allow handling all contingencies in the same way, different simulation methods are applied to different regions in function of the data available. Simulation methodologies most commonly employed are mathematical, historical, and scenario or "what-if" analysis.

Mathematical or numerical simulation — which includes Monte Carlo methods, binomial and trinomial trees, and lattices — is based on a comprehensive probabilistic description of the phenomena to be simulated. This description allows the generation of paths in agreement with probability distributions.

Monte Carlo and tree-based methods are used for solving problems that are mathematically well defined, though they might include parameters that need to be estimated with statistical methods. They assume fundamental sources of randomness and laws that relate this fundamental randomness to the relevant economic variables.

Monte Carlo-type simulation is based on assumptions on probability distributions or on a description of stochastic processes, both of which depend on parameters estimated from historical data. These parameters might be simple volatilities or more complex structures. Whatever, they must be estimated.

Historical simulation, on the other hand, does not make any probability assumptions. It registers what happened in the past and evaluates what might happen in the future in function of the past. Using empirical data, historical simulation builds frequency histograms, quantiles, or equivalent representations. These representations are ultimately probability measures. Though they cannot be formally manipulated mathematically, they are measures of risk and likelihood.

To illustrate the difference between numerical and historical simulation, suppose one holds a portfolio of bonds and derivatives. Using a Monte Carlo method, one has to create a structure of arbitrage-free prices for bonds and derivatives and generate price paths. In generating the paths, sampling is done according to the assumed probability distributions. In this way, a large number of price histories are generated. The probability distribution and, therefore, the risk of the portfolio can be computed observing the distribution of the computed paths.

With historical simulation, no assumptions are made on the probabilistic behavior of the interest rates. One simply observes bond and derivatives prices over some period in the past. Histograms might be computed and different probabilities assigned to different quantiles by counting empirical relative frequencies. These data give the maximum excursion of prices in the period under examination. The maximum loss can then be evaluated taking the worst case of bond prices in the past period. This is the notion of stress analysis: the worst situations that occurred in the past are explored and projected into the future.

Monte Carlo and historical simulation both offer a quantitative measure of risk, albeit with different methodologies and under different assumptions. They can therefore be used for computing confidence intervals, evaluating risk measures such as VaR, and for capital allocation.

Opinions differ on the relative merits of various simulation methods and the limits of applicability. For Frank Lindemann, head of financial engineering at the New York-based software firm Sailfish Systems, a Reuters company, the advantage of historical simulation is that one gets good information on the tail when standard linear assumptions begin to break down. Sailfish Systems uses historical simulation of P&Ls in lieu of probabilistic generation, eschewing the need to write specific mathematical models. Mr. Lindemann remarks that in historical simulation, constraints are not formally imposed by a model but come from the past historical relationships. "The advantage," he says, "is that the world actually happened that way."

Andrew Lapkin, vice president at Bankers Trusts' Raroc Group, takes a different perspective. He remarks that something of the past is useful but that relying on historical simulation alone, one can get pigeon-holed. "Monte Carlo simulation," he says, "relies on, but is not restricted by, the past. It offers some stationarity plus the capability to not follow the last two or three years."

Morgan Stanley's Harry Mendell remarks that his firm uses both Monte Carlo and historical simulation. But Mr. Mendell considers historical simulation the only really sound simulation. "Otherwise," he says, "evaluations remain arbitrary. Who knows the probability of another Gulf War?" Stress testing is also used to find problems that VaR analysis does not identify. Mr. Mendell cites among these the classic risk problem of puts: a trader sells puts; the VaR analysis doesn't find them, but stress testing does.

Within the domain of procedures based on historical data, a distinction can be made between events for which meaningful statistics exist and events that are possible but on which there are not sufficient statistical data. Catastrophes do happen, though rarely. Victor Makarov, at Chase's Client Risk Management Services, remarks that there is not one market risk but two: (1) risk related to business-as-usual and (2) risk related to catastrophic events.

For business-as-usual risk, Dr. Makarov considers VaR analysis the appropriate tool for hedging and allocating capital. As for risk related to catastrophic events, a different tool, namely stress testing, is, he says, required. Dr. Makarov notes that stress testing cannot relate losses to probabilities; it can therefore not be used to hedge as correlation relationships are not stable; nor can it be used to allocate capital as it cannot say to what extent the allocated capital will protect one. Capital allocation should not, he believes, be used to cover catastrophic events.

To protect against catastrophic events, Dr. Makarov advocates holding global diversified portfolios. To determine the level of diversification needed, he suggests stress testing, using actual catastrophic scenarios from the past (e.g., events in 1987 and 1992). The advantage: objectivity.

Dr. Makarov suggests three rules in applying stress testing: (1) use those catastrophes that affect your positions, (2) collect information for all markets for the same period of time, and (3) determine the length of the interval, i.e., where does the catastrophe end? How long a catastrophic event lasts is related to the illiquidity of the market; a catastrophe ends when liquidity comes back.

Scenario simulations are simulations of another sort. Scenario or what-if analysis is used to understand the consequences of assuming a given set of events, irrespective of whether or not the events ever happened. Without reference to historical data, scenario simulation computes the value of financial quantities in scenarios that are possible but to which no probability estimate can be attached. These scenarios might be interest rates jumps, twists, market crashes, particularly adverse prepayments, or other.

In building scenarios, deterministic constraints are imposed, limiting the number of possible scenarios. The range of variations of parameters also needs to be set. Determining scenarios is a judgemental process: today's science can not tell us what scenarios are plausible. Michael Winchell, senior managing director in charge of risk management at Bear Stearns asks, "Do summary measures tell us anything regarding catastrophic loss if our scenarios are not as we imagine or constrain them?"

2.12 THE LIMITS OF VALIDITY OF FINANCE THEORY

Finance theory as it is known today is not an experimentally validated science such as physics. It is a theory of how the market should behave given certain constraints. The level of empirical validation of finance theory is quite modest by current scientific standards. While there is consensus on this point, opinions vary as to how to cope with the shortcomings of today's models. A number of our interviewees expressed caution on the theoretical underpinnings of risk management.

There are several considerations to be made. The first regards financial modeling in general. Finance theory makes a number of assumptions that might be far from reality. The crux of the problem is that there is no such thing as a finance theory, only different models and different levels of assumption.

The most general assumptions are both very general and very robust, but have limited applicability in their sweeping generality. This has been remarked in reference to the no-arbitrage principle. A robust hypothesis, problems arise in applying no-arbitrage models that make important additional simplifications, such as constant volatility. In discussing the validity of finance theory, one is forced to make a distinction between the validity in principle of very broad theories and the practical validity of approximate models.

David Shimko, formerly professor of finance at the University of Southern California and presently head of risk management research at J.P. Morgan, remarks that he now has doubts about the framework of infinitely capitalized markets that he taught when at university. There is, he says, one major difficulty: unlike a physical model, e.g., objects falling in space, there is friction that drives the financial markets. Dr. Shimko notes a complete phase difference between looking at perfect markets and markets with imperfections. He advocates starting with the imperfections: assume that capital is limited and, based on limited capital, ask the question "What can we expect?"

Emanuel Derman, head of the quantitative strategies group at Goldman Sachs and co-developer of the Black-Derman-Toy interest-rate model, was trained as a theoretical particle physicist. Dr. Derman remarks that people coming from a physics background often ask questions like "How do you know when your model is right?" and "How do you check your models?" But finance theory is in many cases not a theory where laws have to be obeyed. "Models," Dr. Derman says, "represent the *dynamics of expectations* rather than the dynamics of what actually comes to pass. Good models give you a set of variables to describe a world and some causal relations between them. They provide a means of thinking about things and conducting gedanken experiments, which are useful in themselves."

Dr. Derman believes that there are different levels of confidence in financial modeling. He notes that in derivatives dealing, although you can model anything at some level of approximation, blind trust should not be placed in the models. "Financial models are," Dr. Derman says, "reference models, suitable for an initial estimate of value which is then amended with common sense and experience." Once amended, the final price is filtered through a model and quoted in Black-Scholes terms.

General approaches to reducing uncertainty related to models are being developed. There are two mathematical strategies. One involves improvements in out-of-sample validation techniques that make more efficient use of validation data; the other involves methodologies for measuring and extrapolating model errors. At Cornell University, Eric Jacquier and Robert Jarrow (1995) developed a generalized framework for evaluating errors in option pricing models. This framework is based on Bayesian statistics augmented with Monte Carlo simulation techniques. Comparing model performance can also give an indication of model validity. Dr. David Gilbert, president of C*ATS Software (Palo Alto, California), remarks that in an effort to reduce model risk, financial firms are making increasing use of externally developed models as a benchmark for internally developed ones.

Andrew Morton, a co-developer of the Heath-Jarrow-Morton interest-rate model and now head of the analytics group for the fixed-income derivatives department at Lehman Brothers, believes that in terms of describing the real world, financial models are not particularly accurate. "But," he says, "if the purpose is to put out a fair value, they are reasonably accurate. Where models are off is for the most part irrelevant." In looking at P&L, Dr. Morton believes that present models are fairly accurate to the first order. "There are," he says, "no big surprises, only little ones."

Dr. Morton identifies a number of areas of progress in modeling. On the derivatives side of their business, where the option pricing theory is fundamental to all they do, he points to advances in refining and estimating models, including the Heath-Jarrow-Morton model. In the area of hedging, Dr. Morton observes that a good deal of emphasis is now on optimal hedging with transaction costs, something the Black-Scholes formulation does not take into consideration. He notes, however, that these refinements have not yet worked their way into the industry.

Another advance Dr. Morton identifies is the rational theory of equilibrium in competitive markets, e.g., arbitrage pricing. The problem, he remarks, is that recent variations on the notion of arbitrage-free involve too many subtleties in the martingale measure for today's crude models. Dr. Morton cites the cost of computational resources as a general limitation to the modeling effort.

There are other aspects of model validity, including the interplay between analytics and data and between theory and intuition and judgement. As for the former, Richard Klotz, partner in charge of the global risk management group at Coopers & Lybrand, comments that because it is never possible to get 100% of the positions in a model, any model will "run afoul" sooner or later.

For Ton Vorst, professor of finance at Erasmus University Rotterdam, there is the need to develop risk management systems that are robust to what you put in them. He cautions against models that might be too sophisticated. If a system depends too much on the input and is not sufficiently robust, the theory, Prof. Vorst argues, has gone too far. He advocates a return to simpler, more robust models.

Are new levels of complexity better? Dr. Klotz remarks that traders build up intuition for any model; if novelty is introduced, the trader has to re-arrange his intuition. Dr. Klotz argues that unless a model allows to price securities materially better, the loss of intuition that its introduction might entail may not be a good thing. Some traders, he adds, are nevertheless quite sophisticated. The need to apply model simplicity constraints must be weighed against the need to capture uncertainty in the world.

Commenting on the implementation of theory in industry, Yu Zhu, director of risk assessment and control at Sakura Global Capital in New York, says that the issue is how to apply the theory. He notes that, while Markowitz's portfolio theory was first defined in 1952, more than 40 years later most financial firms do not yet have a strong concept of portfolio management. As for risk management, Dr. Zhu observes that before the 1987 crash, even major Wall Street firms had no notion of measuring risk: trading losses were often attributed to "unauthorized trading." Though Wall Street was a leading force in developing arbitrage theory, relating risk and return is still an unresolved problem. However, Dr. Zhu attributes the success of major Wall Street firms to their having built up effective risk management systems over the past decade.

Lastly, there is the question of the bottom-line ability of risk management modeling to perform its task accurately. Thomas Daula, a managing director of global risk management at Bankers Trust, remarks that risk management systems try to perform two functions: (1) characterize the relationship between underlying financial variables, such as interest rates and prices, and the values of an institution's positions, i.e., define the institution's trading P&L function and (2) estimate how likely it is that outcomes in various ranges will occur. Mr. Daula remarks that although our understanding of the relationship between these underlying variables and the values of complex financial instruments is constantly improving, the need to recalibrate pricing models is an indication that the models are still only approximately correct. "The need to continuously recalibrate these models is," he says, "a reflection of their limitations."

Mr. Daula does, however, believe that we are moving towards a finer structure of representations and a more econometric approach to characterizing the P&L function. But, he adds, it is hard to get formal models to solve all the problems: they are always just a "caricature of reality." This leads to practical questions of how far formulas should be pushed. Clinton Lively, senior managing director of global risk management at Bankers Trust, thinks that it is necessary to arrive at some quantification of the sensitivity of the results to the underlying assumptions. "Is the framework valid?" he asks.

Alexander Wolfgring, head of risk management and ALCO support at Bank Austria, adds another perspective to the question of model validity. He remarks that their balance sheet and ALM models do not use an overly sophisticated system of interest rates. According to Mr. Wolfgring, this allows them to use a long history — some four years — of interest-rate position data. He would consider problematic the need to recalibrate models more than once a year as it would make it difficult to compare historical data. For Austria's No. 1 bank, the ability to compare its own historical data is more important than gaining a 5% or 10% advantage through more sophisticated models.

References

Aoki, Masanao, *New Approaches to Macroeconomic Modeling*, Cambridge University Press, New York, NY, 1996.

Bernstein, Peter L., *Capital Ideas: The Improbable Origins of Modern Wall Street*, The Free Press, New York, NY, 1992.

Crnkovic, Cedomir and Jordan Drachman, "A Universal Tool to Discriminate Among Risk Measurement Techniques," *Risk Magazine*, September 1996.

Derman, Emanuel, "Model Risk," *Risk Magazine*, vol. 9, no. 5, May 1996.

Duffie, Darrell, *Dynamic Asset Pricing Theory*, Princeton University Press, Princeton, NJ, 1992.

Fabozzi, Frank J., Franco Modigliani and Michael G. Ferri, *Foundations of Financial Markets and Institutions*, Prentice Hall, Englewood Cliffs, NJ, 1994.

Focardi, Sergio and Caroline Jonas, *Modeling the Market: New Theories and Techniques*, Frank J. Fabozzi Associates, New Hope, PA, 1997.

Jacquier, Eric and Robert Jarrow, "Vital Statistics," *Risk Magazine*, vol. 8, no. 4, April 1995.

Jamshidian, Farshid, "Libor and Swap Market Models and Measures," Sakura Global Capital, January 1996.

Jarrow, Robert A. and Stuart Turnbull, "Pricing Derivatives on Financial Securities Subject to Credit Risk," *The Journal of Finance*, vol. L, no. 1, March 1995.

Jarrow, Robert A. and Dilip B. Madan, "Arbitrage, Rational Bubbles, and Martingale Measures," Working Paper, Johnson Graduate School of Management, Cornell University, 1996.

Jarrow, Robert A., *Modelling Fixed Income Securities and Interest Rate Options*, McGraw Hill, New York, NY, 1996.

Lux, Thomas, "Time-variation of Second Moments from a Multi-agent Noise Trader Model of Financial Markets," Second International Conference on Computing in Economics and Finance, Geneva, 1996.

Magill, Michael and Martine Quinzii, *The Theory of Incomplete Markets*, The MIT Press, Cambridge, MA, 1996.

Merton, Robert C., *Continuous-Time Finance*, Blackwell, Cambridge, MA, 1993.

Mueller, U.A., M.M. Dacorogna, R.D. Davé, O.V. Pictet, R.B. Olsen and R.J. Ward, "Fractals and Intrinsic Time — A Challenge to Econometricians," Olsen & Associates, UAM.1993.08-16, Zurich.

Sargent, Thomas J., *Macroeconomics*, Academic Press, San Diego, CA, 1987.

Sharpe, William F., "Nuclear Financial Economics," Research Paper no. 1275, Stanford University Graduate School of Business, November 1993.

Chapter 3

Measuring Risk

3.1 THE RISK MEASUREMENT PROCESS

Our inability to accurately forecast changes in the value of portfolios of assets is the source of financial risk. Pricing and risk management are related: measuring risk is measuring the size and probabilistic features of possible future changes in price. Just what can be considered a sound measure of risk has been much debated. Before exploring today's measures of risk, let's take a look at the risk measurement process.

From the conceptual and practical standpoint, the measurement of risk requires the evaluation of the probability distribution of a portfolio's value. We might be interested in the probability distribution at a specific date or, more in general, at each instant in a specific time interval. The basic notion in risk measurement is therefore that of a stochastic process that represents a portfolio's value. The information contained in the probability distributions of this process is subsequently collapsed into a small set of risk measures.

The risk measurement process consists in choosing models of financial markets, fitting the models to historical data, and applying them to new data. The result is a set of probability distributions from which summary risk measures are computed. Figure 3.1 represents the steps of the risk management process. Data play a role in all phases, including model selection and integration.

A number of conceptual considerations are in order. These include:

- if and how market constraints are to be applied,
- statistical hypotheses,
- the number and type(s) of independent sources of uncertainty,
- the availability of data in function of the models used,
- outliers,
- risk measures, and
- the integration of risk measures.

Figure 3.1

The risk measurement process consists in selecting and integrating models, fitting the models to historical data, and applying them to new data.

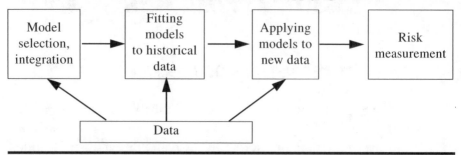

These considerations translate into trade-offs between the availability of data, the complexity of models, and approximations.

It should be noted that all models are in some sense wrong because misspecified. They entail approximations that need to be evaluated in function of available data and the objectives of the risk management exercise. Making explicit these approximations is part of the risk manager's job.

Finance theory provides only relative evaluation methodologies through option theory. To project the probability distribution of a portfolio's returns over a given period, the constraints of finance theory are combined with statistical estimates of the basic risk determinants. Factor analysis and macroeconomic reasoning might be used to provide additional constraints that further reduce the number of independent risk factors to be predicted.

This process entails forecasting. By forecasting is meant not the sure point prediction of rates and prices, but the evaluation of probability distributions over given time horizons; it is the evaluation of how fundamental uncertainties project over economic variables.

The explicit consideration of the theoretical framework is important for two reasons. The first is internal consistency. Often software from different sources is employed. These programs might not use the same analytics; they might be based on different theoretical frameworks. Putting these together might result in inconsistencies. If, for instance, one makes the assumption of normality of distributions and then uses some nonlinear pricing relationships, the process is clearly inconsistent.

The second is a question of understanding the applicability of models in function of the data available. Approximations must be consistent. Sophisticated algorithms might not be appropriate if gross simplifications are made further on. And if data for calibration are lacking, the use of complex models should be avoided as they may not be robust to approximations. The human element must also be taken into consideration. Models must be understood and reflect the prevailing economic views of the firm.

There are also theoretical issues related to just what market constraints to apply. This amounts to deciding on the type and extent of finance theory to apply. Numerous approaches exist. The least theoretically binding is historical simulation, i.e., projecting historical statistical data to the future. This approach eschews assumptions on the relationship between variables.

Growing sets of constraints can be applied. The basic market law in risk management — the no-arbitrage principle — translates into different modeling options and is subject to different levels of approximation. There is, for example, a wide choice of models of the term structure of interest rates. One might adopt constant volatilities or stochastic volatilities. Stochastic volatility, in turn, can be modeled by different processes including a variety of X-ARCH models. In addition, one might consider first or second-order approximations to the theoretical relationships between derivatives and the underlyings. The above raises difficult questions as theoretical constraints are valid only within certain representations of financial markets and might not be mutually consistent.

Constraints may be not only relationships between variables but also assumptions on the shape of probability distributions. Many systems assume normal distributions, which are common in nature. The reason is contained in a theorem of probability theory which states that the sum of many small independent random variables is approximately normal even if every variable is not normal. What is important is that no variable is predominant and that the variables are (at least weakly) independent. Consequently, phenomena that depend on many small independent factors can be assumed to be normal; a portfolio that depends on many small independent price processes can be assumed to be normally distributed.

The assumption that all distributions are normal implies that relationships between variables are linear. Any linear combination of normal variables is normal. If there are nonlinear relationships, distributions cannot, generally speaking, all be normal. The original Risk-Metrics assumption of normality implies the consideration of only first-order linear approximations to relationships between variables.

But portfolio probability distributions typically depend on factors that are not independent and that are characterized by nonlinear relationships, such as the relationship between derivatives prices and the price of their underlyings. The assumption of normality is therefore an approximation whose validity needs to be checked in function of a given portfolio. Recent editions of Risk-Metrics allow to handle nonlinearities to account for optionality.

From the mathematical point of view, assumptions on probability distributions and market constraints are two sides of a coin. Ultimately, we are interested in modeling probability distributions. In finance, there are a number of relationships that we believe are reasonable though they carry some uncertainty. To handle this uncertainty, we add an uncertainty term to basic relationships. In modeling the price behavior of stocks, for instance, we find it reasonable to believe that prices grow exponentially. But we are uncertain about this growth, so we add a Brownian motion as a random disturbance.

It would be possible to take a different conceptual approach, modeling probability distributions upfront. This leads to differential equations. The two approaches are basically equivalent: a number of relationships link random variables and, therefore, probability distributions. Whether we think of them as sure relationships with added disturbances or as links between probability distributions does not make much difference.

What is important is understanding the approximations and simplifications made in the process. Finance theory is a general framework that can be applied to virtually any market. In applying theory, simplifications are made. As a result, the theory fits the data only approximately. The consistency and implications of this approximation process have to be checked.

Some approximations and their consequences are easy to grasp. The assumption of normality — which implies the assumption of linearity in the relationships between variables — is easy to understand. Other approximations might be less transparent. An example is the inconsistencies between Libor and swap interest-rate measures found by Farshid Jamshidian (see 2.4).

Another point, related to the above, is determining the number of independent sources of uncertainty to admit in a system. The end result of applying theoretical constraints is that the entire set of risky variables can be expressed in terms of a smaller set of variables that can be considered the primary risk determinants. How many primary variables are required? Is a parsimonious system more or less accurate than a system that includes a large set of variables? There is a trade-off between the number of independent variables and the power of the theory.

In equity portfolio management, the CAPM (Capital Asset Pricing Model) theory proposed using only one variable, the beta, while APT (Arbitrage Pricing Theory) systems such as software developer BARRA's take into account tens of independent risk factors. Global risk management systems such as J.P. Morgan's RiskMetrics are based on hundreds of basic rates that generate a large variance-covariance matrix. Early models of the term structure of interest rates used only one factor; more recent (multifactor) models can handle many.

Does explanatory power increase with the number of factors considered? Why then do we do factor analysis? What do we gain or lose in factor analysis? That we can reasonably ask these questions is an indication of the fact that we do not have a true theory of risk management, but simply adopt a suite of models in function of needs. There are practical consequences.

The aim of science is to arrive at the most parsimonious description possible of a phenomenon. Ideally, the objective is to establish a small number of axioms from which all the complexities of a phenomenon can be derived by chains of logical deductions. The physical sciences have been able to condense the description of the physical world into an amazingly small number of quantities and laws.

But there is a caveat. Science has condensed the description of the laws of nature, but the description of actual portions of nature can be very complex. The laws that govern the motion of fluids, for example, can be stated in formulas that occupy not more than a page. But to describe the motion of an actual plane, the amount of data required is truly formidable. Science has therefore achieved a high level of simplification in the statement of laws, but has left complexity in the actual description of artifacts. An effort is under way to link the two by understanding what complexities are implied or explained by basic laws. This is the subject of the theory of complex systems.

There is no easy compromise between the detailed description of large-scale objects and the simplicity of laws. The economy and financial markets are truly complex objects. Simple all-encompassing laws describing them can not yet be isolated. The no-arbitrage principle comes closest to a true law of the markets, but it is limited in scope.

In describing financial markets, we make compromises. If we adopt a large number of descriptive parameters, we might arrive at a more accurate description of the economy in some region. In doing so, however, we lose the ability to understand phenomena and quickly run short of data to calibrate and validate our models. If we adopt a mathematically binding but inaccurate theory, on the other hand, we might make gross mistakes.

The attractiveness of the CAPM model is due to its ability to explain the behavior of stocks in terms of only one parameter. But this parameter is elusive and difficult to compute and the CAPM description only approximate. More parameters are therefore taken into account. This requires many independent measurements of the parameters used. As a consequence, models must be specialized for different geographies and economic blocks, each with its own set of parameters.

If one can establish well validated laws that entail only a few factors, he or she achieves a high predictive capability. But there is no rule that might give an a priori indication of the optimal number of variables. The process entails refinement guided by a compromise between the amount of data available and the ability to understand the models.

Very few organizations attempt to do true factor analysis in risk management though major Wall Street firms are using massively parallel computers for data analysis. Understanding the factors that affect each line of business and finding a parsimonious set of relationships is a formidable task that requires considerable resources. It is the task, says Harry Mendell, vice president in firm risk management at Morgan Stanley, that is absorbing most of their computational resources.

3.2 PRICING AND RISK MEASUREMENT

"If you can price it, you can hedge it," remarks Andrew Morton, head of the analytics group for the fixed-income derivatives department at Lehman Brothers. This deceptively simple statement underlines the close relationship between pricing and risk management.

At the heart of risk management is the probability distribution of the value of portfolios in the future. To estimate the value of a portfolio, an estimate of the price of the securities held is needed. The pricing methodology thus becomes the basis of the risk management methodology, allowing to determine the future stochastic evolution of computed prices in function of the underlyings that act as determinants. It also allows to engineer hedging strategies.

An important aspect of pricing is the ability to build a common framework that ties together market prices. This framework is currently provided by the no-arbitrage principle which sets the conditions that all prices must respect and brings them under the umbrella of option pricing theory. The no-arbitrage principle has important consequences: it allows to value securities that might not be found easily in the market. Still more important, it allows to project prices into the future, linking them to risk factors.

In principle, one could eschew the use of pricing models in risk management, simply applying statistical estimates. This modeling option is provided by historical simulation, which does not assume any pricing methodology but simply projects statistical estimates of portfolio values.

If pricing models are used, prices have to be projected into the future. Farshid Jamshidian, head of product development and strategic trading at Sakura Global Capital in London, remarks that there are two separate components in risk measurement: (1) valuation models and (2) simulation models. With valuation models, the concern is the value today. An important component of valuation models is yield curve generation, the objective being a smooth forward interest-rate curve.

As for simulation models, Dr. Jamshidian remarks that the question is how to generate realistic curve scenarios. If the price distribution has to be computed at some future date, one must have realistic models of the interest-rate curve at each moment. In general, there will be an entire set of curves that needs to be generated.

What is the relationship between the accuracy of pricing methodologies and risk measurement? If the pricing process is uncertain, what are the implications for risk measurement?

Richard Klotz, partner in charge of the global financial risk management group of Coopers & Lybrand, remarks that the risk management process is less model dependent than the pricing process. "It is," he says, "easier for models to agree on changes in prices than on initial prices." To illustrate the point, imagine that two pricing algorithms compute the price of a security at $90 and $100 respectively, a $10 difference. If, however, a 5% price change is projected over a given horizon, the difference of this projection for the two prices is 50 cents.

There is also the fundamental issue of the validity of the pricing mechanism. Bankers Trust senior managing director of global risk management Clinton Lively believes that there is the need to re-evaluate the assumed level of certainty within the framework. Ultimately, arriving at an industry standard on certainty implies solving the problem of the robustness of representations.

Mr. Lively does not see in the making any theoretical advance capable of reducing uncertainty. Expectations are set assuming the validity of the pricing techniques used. But, Mr. Lively notes, there is uncertainty on the techniques and thus intrinsic uncertainty in the pricing process.

3.3 FAT TAILS AND EXTREME EVENTS

Some portfolios of financial assets show complex probabilistic behavior with relatively large risk concentrated in small regions. The probability distributions of these portfolios do not behave like normal distributions but present a concentration of risk in areas far from the average, i.e., in the tails of the distribution that are "fat" with respect to a normal distribution.

Fat tails reflect the occurrence of extreme events that can happen more frequently than Gaussian models suggest. "What kills you," remarks Gary Gastineau, head of new product development at the American Stock Exchange, "is not what occurs one time in 20, but one or two times in 1000 when you expect it only one time in 100,000."

The consideration of tail behavior is important for pricing risk, optimizing returns, and ensuring the survival of the firm. Fat tails are related to linearity in evaluating positions: if a variable depends linearly on a normal variable, then it is itself normal. If one admits non-linear relationships between variables, then non-normal distributions have to be considered. Robert Jarrow, professor of investment management at Cornell University's Johnson Graduate School of Management, remarks that normality is too simplistic and not even close to a reasonable approximation. He advocates a more general perspective that should consider nonlinearities and non-normalities.

To understand the concept of fat tails, it is useful to begin by considering a normal distribution. The bulk of events is distributed within a region around the expected value. In regions far from the expected value, say beyond some multiple of variance, probabilities become negligible. If we translate this distribution into time behavior, we find fluctuations around an average that become very rare when large. If the distribution is sharp, values are concentrated around the expected value. The time evolution shows small fluctuations around the average, with large fluctuations rare to the point of being negligible.

Suppose one adds to a sharp distribution some distant small probability peak, i.e., a fat tail. Values concentrate around some average, but there is a small though not negligible area concentrated around some large value. Translating this probability distribution into time behavior, one would find a stable sequence of values around some average plus occasional large deviations. Stock market indexes behave in this way (see Campbell, Lo, and MacKinlay, 1997).

The consideration of tail behavior might present significant problems to estimating and testing when at the limits of very rare events. Consider events whose probabilities correspond to a frequency of once every one hundred years. There is no way to empirically test behavior of this type. Still, these events might be significant. In most cases, the consideration of such events is done through business judgement, assigning probability measures to outliers in function of a qualitative assessment.

From the analytical point of view, there are several ways to evaluate outliers. One approach is to take some multiple of the standard deviation. In doing so, one extrapolates the distribution function. The pitfall here is that there is no real knowledge of probability distributions outside of the areas where statistically meaningful data are available. Intuition and judgement must then be applied. Andrew Lapkin of Bankers Trust's Raroc Group remarks that to understand outliers and extreme events, they look at two or three standard deviation moves. In the process of handling extreme events, however, he underlines the need to apply judgement.

There are interesting developments in the area of extrapolation and the representation of tail behavior. While is not possible to make quantitative estimates of probability relative to extreme events, it might be possible to create extrapolations based on causal laws validated in other ranges of probabilities. The novelty here is in improvements in extrapolation due to a careful consideration of causal links. As illustrated in Figure 3.2, a global problem is decomposed into subproblems that are more tractable statistically speaking. Adverse combinations of events are then considered and their consequences evaluated.

Figure 3.2

To allow the handling of extreme events, problems are decomposed into statistically meaningful subproblems and extrapolated through adverse causal links; the results are then projected over extreme events.

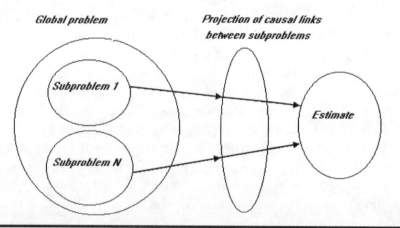

Paul Embrechts, professor of applied probability and insurance mathematics at the Swiss Federal Institute of Technology-Zurich, remarks that handling outliers in financial data will remain a difficult issue. Any solution, he says, will need to combine the best possible tools for looking at the data, technical estimates under well defined given conditions, and stress scenarios. He believes that modern extreme value theory offers valuable tools for finance in general and for risk management in particular.

Prof. Embrechts cites the handling of two extreme events, the Dutch dyke disaster and the Challenger explosion. Following the breaking of the sea dykes in 1953, the Dutch government set up the Delta-committee with the mandate to estimate the necessary dyke heights so as to prevent future flooding with a sufficiently high probability. The government established that the probability of flooding should be less than one in 10,000 years. Clearly, insufficient historical data were available against a 10,000-year goal. To solve the problem, an extrapolation procedure for estimating well beyond the range of available data was called for. This procedure made optimal use of the data available.

The Challenger explosion, remarks Prof. Embrechts, shows another side of the problem of extreme events: the available data has to be looked at very critically, and communication between all levels in an organization has to be safeguarded. From the ex-post analysis of the Challenger failure done by the late Richard Feynman, Nobel prize-winning physicist, it emerges that data were not looked at critically and that figures were chosen so that when added up they gave the 1 in 100,000 probability estimate management wanted. In addition, communication on key issues was far from optimal.

"Extreme value theory," Prof. Embrechts says, "does not provide a miracle cure for questions concerning extreme events; it does, however, provide a well understood set of techniques that are essential in analyzing questions concerning VaR and beyond, i.e., not just the frequency of a particular loss but also the severity." These methods, he adds, are better than various ad hoc methods still in use.

Prof. Embrechts is a co-founder of Risklab, a joint venture between the Swiss Federal Institute of Technology-Zurich and major Swiss financial institutions to undertake precompetitive research on risk management.

Another aspect of the handling of extreme events is their pricing. How, for instance, can one price the credit risk associated with a triple-A rating which is beyond statistical measurement? There is clearly a conventional element involved. Pricing is done by comparison with more statistically significant situations. One starts with pricing events that correspond to meaningful statistics and applies increments in a consistent way. The key is to consider transition probabilities between conventional measures of risk, creating a probability transition matrix for ratings. This matrix gives the probability of transition between different ratings.

Perhaps the most important of rare events are sudden large-scale market movements or *catastrophes*. There is the need to arrive at a deeper understanding of their economic meaning. Understanding catastrophes in quantitative terms is not easy: it involves the modeling of systems far from a state of equilibrium. Catastrophes are not provoked by a coherent shift of consensus on market prices; they are a sort of chain reaction, often initiated and led by minor market participants. A number of participants cannot sustain — even temporarily — big losses and liquidate their positions. Others ride the wave out, eventually trying to make a profit. "We are," Prof. Jarrow says, "in the Dark Ages as regards understanding how to protect ourselves against swellings."

Very large movements or catastrophes have some peculiar characteristics. They are temporary and affect only some geographies and market sectors. In a sense, they can be considered pathologies as they are triggered by a combination of events, reach a peak, and then return to some *steady state* after a period.

In a number of post-catastrophe cases, business is simply resumed at the pre-catastrophe levels. In other cases, however, there are structural changes in the economy. The structure of prices might, for instance, be altered. There is a need to understand, in economic terms, if large movements will make deep structural instability surface or if they will simply "clean" the system.

Victor Makarov, vice president of Chase's Client Risk Management Services, remarks that to properly determine risk capital one should be able to measure risk and forecast distributions. With today's methods, however, this is not possible for catastrophic events: we are unable to develop a model that includes both noise and big movements. Dr. Makarov argues that large swings cannot be forecast with statistical methodologies: there are too few observations and these movements involve deep structural changes in the economy.

Dr. Makarov adds that the failure to understand that if one cannot forecast fat tails one cannot forecast distributions puts excessive demands on capitalization, leading to over-capitalization. He advocates diversification as an effective risk management tool against catastrophic events. Tanya Styblo Beder, principal of New York-based Capital Market Risk Advisors, concurs. "You can put all your eggs in one basket," she says, "only if you can afford to lose all your eggs."

3.4 SINGLE-NUMBER RISK MEASURES AND THE PITFALLS

The entire set of probability distributions is the most complete description of risk in a probabilistic setting. It might, however, be too complex even for automated treatment. To simplify the measurement of risk, the information contained in probability distributions is generally collapsed into small sets of numbers that give a summary representation of risk. Risk measures are commonly summarized in one of two ways: (1) as parameters that allow an approximate quantitative characterization of probability distributions and (2) as the probability of specific events. We will first look at these, then at sensitivity ratios and lastly, more in general, at how to assign risk measures to spaces of outcomes.

No quantity can be considered the *correct* measure of risk. Each measure serves some purpose. It might be used to allocate capital, to evaluate the global level of risk, or to optimize. The merits of a measure are related to the objectives of the risk measurement process. A risk measure is "good" if it serves its purpose.

The most common summary characterization of distributions are variance and covariance. Variance is the expected value of the square of a random variable; covariance is the expected value of the product of the deviations of two random variables from their respective averages. These numbers are a characterization of the shape of probability distributions and of joint probability distributions. Variances reveal if distributions are highly concentrated or if they spread over a large set of possible values. Covariances reveal if variables move together or if a large range of combinations of values can be found. If distributions are concentrated in small regions, we have a lot of information about the future. The amount of risk is therefore limited. If, however, distributions are spread out, there is a high degree of uncertainty.

   To give an intuitive feeling for risk measures, it is appropriate to recall how probability translates into the time statistics of a realization of a financial series, assuming stationarity. Suppose that there is a time series $x = x(t)$ in discrete or continuous time. The probability that x is in a given interval, i.e., $p(a \leq x \leq b)$ for given a and b is approximated by the time that the series spends in that interval divided by the total time under observation. Figure 3.3 illustrates this concept.

Figure 3.3
Risk as measured by variance: the width of the curve measures the size of the risk.

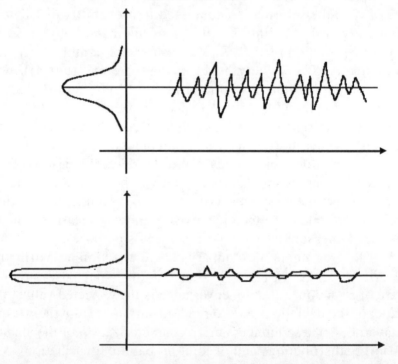

As variance is interpreted and computed taking the successive values of a time series, variance also represents the volatility of the corresponding quantity, i.e., it is related to the size and frequency of the movements of the same quantity. But variance offers an indication only of the *magnitude* of the excursion that can be expected. This is because the same variance can be generated by a few large movements or by frequent small ones. In fact, a given variance is compatible with infinite different time evolutions of the series under consideration.

At Goldman Sachs, Fisher Black and Robert Litterman developed a generalized approach to risk management based on a variance-covariance matrix. In his article "Hot Spots and Hedges," Mr. Litterman (1996) emphasizes the benefit of a simple analytical approach in risk management, underlining the powerful insight that can be gained from linear approximations when valid.

An important finding about variance is that volatility, i.e., variance, tends to cluster in time. An analysis of many economic time series has shown that there are periods of high volatility followed by periods of low volatility. This behavior, called heteroschedasticity, is captured by the ARCH and GARCH models. Variance-based risk management models are beginning to take heteroschedasticity into account in forecasting variance.

Another approach to single-number measures of risk is the evaluation of the confidence interval. Confidence intervals specify events associated with a certain probability. The most common measure of risk based on confidence intervals is value-at-risk (VaR). VaR is the maximum loss that might happen *within a certain confidence interval*, i.e., within a specified probability limit.

The term VaR might be misleading. It does not tell us what the maximum possible loss is, but only that there is a certain probability that losses will exceed a specified amount. Suppose we say that there is a VaR of $1mn with a 95% confidence interval. This means that there is a 5% probability that losses will exceed $1mn or, equivalently, a 95% probability of losses less than $1mn. If we consider a one-day horizon this means that, on the average, every 100 days losses will exceed $1mn in five of those days. VaR, however, does not specify the amount of possible losses outside of the confidence interval (see Figure 3.4).

Figure 3.4

Risk as measured by VaR; the shaded area represents a confidence interval, in this case 95%. The shape of the probability distribution to the left of the shaded area is not specified.

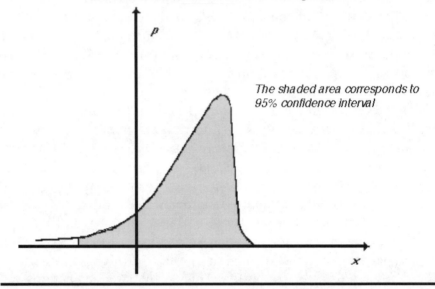

The shaded area corresponds to 95% confidence interval

Computing VaR does not depend on the assumption that a distribution is Gaussian. It is possible to compute VaR — and variance — for any distribution. However, if a distribution is Gaussian, both VaR and variance are sufficient, if taken together with expected values, to completely characterize a distribution. In fact, a Gaussian distribution depends mathematically on only two parameters.

If distributions are not Gaussian, measuring risk through single numbers is much less effective as there might be a concentration of rare events in some small region that is not revealed by VaR or variance. In VaR terms, outside of the confidence interval there might be significant events with a relatively high probability of occurring.

Taking the above VaR example, the 5% residual probability of losses in excess of $1mn might all be concentrated in the region of, say, $10 mn. This means that every 100 days, there might be five days where losses are in this range. Behavior of this type, with large losses concentrated in small regions, is not infrequent in financial markets. Gary Gastineau, head of new product development at the American Stock Exchange, underlines the need to make sure that what you are modeling matters. He questions whether the 95% confidence interval is what matters and adds, "What's important is how you handle tails and options."

Neither VaR nor variance provides any information about correlations. Knowing the VaRs or variances of two portfolios, one has no knowledge of their correlations or of how their risks combine. More problematic, the VaR of combined portfolios might well exceed the sum of their respective VaRs. To illustrate this, imagine that one has two portfolios with a VaR of $1mn each. This means that over 100 days, in 95 days losses are below $1mn for each portfolio. But this does not mean that losses of the combined portfolio are less than $2 mn for 95 days because of the effect of losses in the remaining five days.

For Alexander Wolfgring, head of risk management and ALCO support at Bank Austria, correlations are the weak point of VaR. The Vienna-based bank uses sensitivity analysis to analyze the effect of changing correlations on risk measurement results.

VaR has become a widely used measure of risk. There are many reasons for its popularity. It is recommended by the regulators. It is the key concept in the widely diffused J.P. Morgan RiskMetrics approach to quantifying market risk. Taken at the firmwide level, VaR has the merit of being relatively intuitive and easy to understand as a global measure of risk; variance seems more abstract. But VaR being only one measure of risk, a sound evaluation of risk requires a more complete set of measurements. In particular, both stress analysis and correlation analysis need to be performed.

There are other shortcomings in VaR-type risk measurement. Michael Winchell, senior managing director in charge of risk management at Bear Stearns, points out that VaR does not provide insight into "how" to manage a business, i.e., it doesn't provide a map of action if the manager believes that the VaR is too large. "There is," Mr. Winchell says, "no corollary between a big VaR and how big one wants to be in the business."

A number of our interviewees remarked that VaR measures are ambiguously defined from a practical standpoint. Tanya Styblo Beder, principal of Capital Market Risk Advisors, describes herself as a fan of VaR, but not of all the confidence placed in it. In her article "VaR: Seductive but Dangerous," Ms. Beder (1995) demonstrates that computing VaR with different methodologies might yield significantly different results.

VaR and variance characterize probability distributions in the absolute sense. Relative measures of risk are used as ratios between different quantities. They show how changes in parameters are reflected in price changes. In equity analysis, a portfolio's beta reveals how the portfolio reacts to changes in the market portfolio. In the APT model, a number of coefficients reveal how equity prices vary in function of the respective factors. For derivatives portfolios, the Greeks are sensitivity measures that show how derivative prices change in function of changes in the underlyings. Sensitivity ratios are a mathematical device to project the uncertainty of some variable over other variables.

The Greeks are widely used at major Wall Street firms. A plus of the methodology is that it is computationally tractable; a minus is that as the value of the underlying changes, the value of the Greeks also changes: linearity is not constant. One of our interviewees remarked that they "march through history" with stress testing, changing the Greeks to see what happens.

Other ratios are used to reveal sensitivity to interest rates. In fixed income, duration measures how the value of a bond portfolio changes in function of parallel shifts of interest rates; convexity measures how the value of a bond portfolio changes in function of the curvature of interest rates.

It is possible to explore in more general terms how to assign a measure of risk to a space of outcomes. Jean-Marc Eber, head of R&D at Société Générale's capital markets division in Paris, remarks there is a need for a sound theoretical framework for thinking about risk measures. He believes that the popularity of VaR as a method for assigning a single number to a position has delayed the appearance of a theoretical framework. In a paper (1996) co-authored with professors Philippe Artzner (University of Strasbourg), Freddy Delbaen (Swiss Federal Institute of Technology-Zurich) and David Heath (Cornell University), an attempt was made to arrive at an axiomatic characterization of the measures of risk. Their work makes no assumptions on probability; good risk measures are defined respecting the constraint to take maximum expected loss on a set of probability distributions.

Mr. Eber remarks that a good risk measure is one which has good aggregation power. He advocates the notion of sub-additivity. The need for sub-additivity is, he says, dictated by the need to decentralize the organization, to give independent limits to different trading desks, and to aggregate procedures. VaR, Mr. Eber adds, is not sub-additive: it enables each unit that calculates its risk measures to throw away its 5% of bad cases.

There are alternatives to single-number risk measures for summarizing risk. Erasmus University's Ton Vorst mentions work in the area of linking risk measures with option pricing theory, an approach he believes will become increasingly important. It is easy, he says, to understand what options do versus risk measures.

Prof. Vorst advocates splitting risk measures into several different parts or books, e.g., bond, option and stock books, each with its own risk measure. A pitfall in using a single-number measure is the focus against a single asset. "You really need to get your correlations right," Prof. Vorst says, "and this is not so easy to do." Because correlations can change, it is, he says, hard to get a hold on the problem.

3.5 MULTIDIMENSIONAL RISK MEASURES

Single-number measures of risk such as VaR have the merit of making risk measurement tractable; they might, however, be inadequate for practical purposes such as hedging or optimization. Risk measurement is a multidimensional process: it entails the parallel consideration of different risk measures that need to be integrated in articulated risk management policies.

Researchers have attempted to extend the scope of risk measurement by considering not single numbers but vectors of numbers. In considering vectors, the global risk picture is represented by the entire set of numbers. This approach has proved fruitful in areas such as interest-rate risk.

A number of multidimensional risk measures have been proposed. Robert Reitano introduced the concept of "partial duration" (1992); Gifford Fong Associates developed the "functional duration" risk measure (see Fabozzi and Fong 1994); Ravi Dattatreya and Frank

Fabozzi (1995) developed the risk point method for measuring the risk of a bond or bond portfolio. The risk point method is a relative risk measure insofar as it measures the risk in a bond or portfolio relative to a specific hedging instrument. The risk point, also called the relative dollar duration, measures the change in the value of a bond or portfolio due to a 1-basis point change in the yield of the hedge instrument in a given maturity sector. To determine a complete risk profile, a full set of risk points relative to a set of hedge instruments is needed.

The concept of duration was extended by Thomas Ho, co-developer of the Ho-Lee interest-rate model and president of GAT. Dr. Ho (1992) introduced the concept of key rate durations, a set of duration measures to characterize not only parallel shifts of the term structure but also changes in its shape. This concept was implemented in the GAT Integrated Bond System (IBS) software.

3.6 VISUALIZING RESULTS

Risk management is based on risk measurements represented as probability distributions. But — with the exception of the simplest cases — probability distributions carry far too much information for humans to handle in decision making. Risk measurement information is therefore typically "collapsed" into a small set of numbers.

An alternative to collapsing information is to represent it visually. If the human brain has difficulty crunching numbers, it does much better as a pattern organizer. In many cases, the brain's ability to process visual information is superior to its ability to process numerical or verbal information. For this reason, much data-rich scientific information is carried in visualization programs run on powerful workstations or supercomputers. Sophisticated visualization techniques are now also being applied to finance and risk management.

Visible Decisions, a Toronto-based software company, developed interactive three-dimensional information visualization applications for analyzing large sets of data (see Figure 3.5). Financial firms such as Morgan Stanley are experimenting with the software as a means of presenting information, allowing for intuitive what-if analysis. Such capability could eventually be put on an internal network or even extended to external sites.

Figure 3.5

Interactive 3-D visualization programs, such as Head Trader by Visible Decisions, allow monitoring in an intuitive way an entire trading floor in real time.

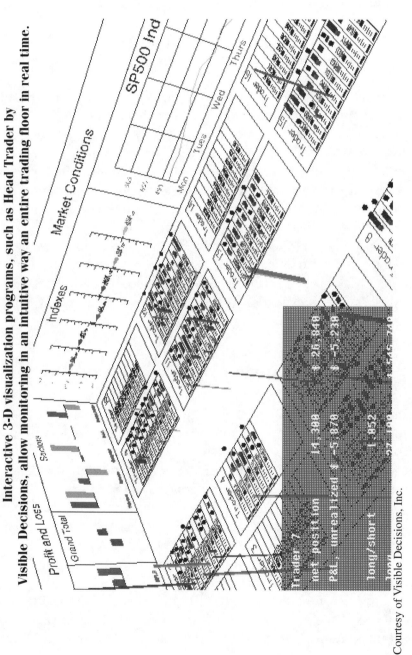

Courtesy of Visible Decisions, Inc.

Michael Winchell, senior managing director for risk management at Bear Stearns, observes that it would be useful to visualize the various Monte Carlo simulations into a "risk terrain" rather than be limited to a summary value. Comparing the visualization of risk management to that used in war games, it would, he says, be useful to "fly over the virtual terrain, seeing the potential deep losses as one would see canyons."

Following a similar line of thinking, BZW Barclays, the investment banking arm of Barclays Bank, formed an alliance with UK military researchers. Together with DERA (Defense Evaluation and Research Agency), BZW developed the description of a system that takes data and converts it into analogue dials to reflect performance. An alternative approach is to create a three-dimensional lattice of shapes with hollows and hills representing equity returns in function of various parameters. The business objective is to even out the terrain, i.e., to reduce risk by buying or selling investments to manage the portfolio. Why did BZW turn to researchers at the military labs? Martin Dooney, head of global money markets at BZW Barclays and project leader, observes that the best visualization techniques he has seen come from the military effort.

3.7 INTEGRATING RISK MEASURES

The methodologies of risk management are not single and all-encompassing. There are different regions of data characterized by different statistical validation techniques. Summary risk measures capture only some aspects of risk. There is the need to integrate different risk measures among themselves and with judgement and intuition.

It is the risk manager's job to design a set of measures that ensure data adequate for the decision-making process. It is also his or her job to integrate these measures. If the firm's objective is not only to comply with regulators but also to optimize the business, these are important tasks.

Integration is particularly difficult when handling different types of risk. Credit and market risk and, eventually, operations risk, present integration challenges. Different statistical behavior, different distributions in time, and different time horizons must be reconciled under the same conceptual and analytical framework. Svein Eidem, general manager in group risk management at Den norske Bank in Oslo, remarks that finding a common measure is a major concern in their effort to integrate market, credit, and operations risk.

Model validity is one of the principal factors responsible for the need to integrate. Clinton Lively, senior managing director of global risk management at Bankers Trust, remarks that validity becomes an implied parameter of the risk management process, but one that is in no way measurable. This, he says, leads to significant risks. The standard framework for what is measurable assumes the validity of pricing models and gives useful information only inside that framework.

Mr. Lively notes that the accent is on understanding positions and getting objective information on prices and price sensitivity. This calls for the use of complementary data sets. Mr. Lively suggests that it is a combination of methods — e.g., VaR and stress testing — that is needed, together with the exercise of management judgement aside the models.

Thomas Daula, a managing director of global risk management at Bankers Trust, underlines the need to understand positions objectively. VaR, he remarks, is just one of the many outputs of a risk management system, each of which provides valuable insights. Mr. Daula notes that many significant risks are related to events that cannot be characterized as draws from a stationary process. It is, for example, difficult to assign probability measures to low-frequency events whose timing and magnitude are often a consequence of political or policy decisions, e.,g., devaluations of managed currencies.

As the integration of risk measures is a judgemental process, it is important that the information used in decision making be consistent with the economic views of the decision makers. A number of our interviewees cited the need to identify the main channels of risk and to decompose portfolios to understand it they are consistent with the company's trading and economic views. Because there are implied views in the analysis, consistency with economic intuition must be checked.

Given that risk management is an inherently multidimensional process with subjective components, how should one act upon risk? "Prudently," says Tanya Styblo Beder, principal of Capital

Market Risk Advisors. "But do not hunt risk down and eliminate it," she adds. "Risk is a source of profit. It's bad when it is unknown or misunderstood." Ms. Beder considers mathematics necessary but not sufficient to managing risk, and advocates a greater use of the experience of senior management in setting the assumptions that go into the models. She suggests doing "what-if-I-am wrong" scenarios.

Lesley Daniels Webster, head of market risk management at Chase Manhattan Bank, remarks that risk management is a question of business judgement, experience, and intuition. "The conscience of the firm," she says, "cannot be automated; there is some information that cannot be abstracted." A high level of scientific grounding is, Ms. Daniels Webster says, required, but the ultimate question is: Does the information the model generates seem reasonable? Does it fit with reality as perceived through experience?

3.8 NUMERICAL METHODS

Numerical methods can be divided into two classes: (1) algorithms for processing large amounts of numerical information and (2) algorithms for the numerical solution of equations expressed in the language of differential mathematics. The two are not necessarily related.

Continuous-time mathematics is a late addition to financial analytical tools. A large part of mathematical finance can, in fact, be formulated in a discrete-time setting. In this setting, which assumes that the economy moves in discrete steps, numerical methods are used to compute the paths of different securities. At each step, there are discrete probability distributions for the next step. If transition probabilities depend on only the current state and not the previous history, the process is called Markovian. Markovian processes are much simpler numerically than non-Markovian processes.

Most results of mathematical finance can be expressed in a discrete-time setting without reference to a continuous-time analogue. Examples include the no-arbitrage principle and the martingale formulation of finance. In the discrete-time setting, numerical methods can be used for valuation purposes under the assumption of market completeness and absence of arbitrage.

In numerical computation, one creates a large number of discrete paths of some basic set of securities according to probability distributions. Other paths are subsequently computed by imposing no-arbitrage constraints expressed through algebraic relationships. From a practical standpoint, a mechanism to compute probabilities is needed. This implies estimating parameters for probability transitions. In binomial trees, for instance, an estimate of up-down transition probabilities is required.

These methodologies are essentially self-contained: no reference to differential formulations is required. Not intended to be an approximation to continuous-time processes, they are simple and require only a limited number of statistical estimates as parameters. Many numerical methods used in finance are of this type. Simulations can be performed without the need to make reference to continuous-time formulations.

There are, however, numerical methods that are an approximation process of some continuous-time formulation. The advantage of continuous-time formulations is two-fold: (1) generality and (2) an enhanced ability to make statistical estimates. Continuous-time formulations allow to express concisely properties that it would be cumbersome or impossible to express in a discrete-time setting. The Black-Scholes formula is a case in point: it gives a simple relationship between price and volatility in continuous time. More in general, one can use a vast body of continuous-time mathematics.

In a continuous-time setting, however, numerical methods are of a greater complexity. The numerical solution of a continuous-time process is a different mathematical object than the simple discrete-time representation of processes. Continuous-time stochastic processes are defined as a set of time-dependent random variables.

Stochastic processes can be described in various ways. One description is through stochastic differential equations; another is through differential equations that constrain the evolution of probability distributions; yet another is the explicit specification of joint probability distributions of random variables at different moments. Each description leads to a different numerical method.

There are four basic numerical methods:

- The first are closed formulas of which the Black-Scholes formula is an example. In a number of cases, it is possible to establish properties of stochastic processes as closed formulas. Formulas are expressions that are considered "known" as they imply only the computation of standard functions such as sines, cosines or normal distributions. In this case, numerical methods are limited to computing basic functions.

- The second method uses trees, binomial or trinomial, as approximations of continuous-time processes. This method is an application of the central-limit theorem.

- The third numerical method involves sampling the underlying stochastic processes, creating a large number of sample paths. Monte Carlo methods belong to this category: they simulate mathematically a random sampling of the stochastic process under study.

- The fourth numerical method is the numerical solution of partial differential equations (PDEs). There is a mathematical correspondence between stochastic differential equations and partial differential equations that drive probability distributions. In fact, Monte Carlo methods are one way of solving PDEs.

Figure 3.6 depicts the inter-relationship between mathematical methods for representing stochastic processes and the corresponding simulation techniques. In representing the evolution of probability distributions, stochastic calculus and integro-differential equations are equivalent methods for large classes of problems.

An important area of overlapping are diffusion processes, i.e., processes that can be described through stochastic equations or, equivalently, through the Fokker-Planck equation. Simulation methods such as Monte Carlo are associated with stochastic calculus while finite difference methods are associated with differential equations. Appendix A.3.1 gives a brief overview of recent developments in simulation methodologies in finance.

Opinions differ as to the merits of the various numerical methods and their practical application. In the equity division of

Goldman Sachs, the preferred techniques are binomial or trinomial trees and partial differential equation solvers. There are few closed-form solutions and most problems are handled numerically. "We attempt to model the world as realistically as possible," Emanuel Derman, head of the quantitative strategies group, remarks. In practice, Dr. Derman adds, most problems they have encountered reduce to one or two-factor problems. For complex situations, Monte Carlo simulation is either the first or the last resort.

Mark Garman, emeritus professor of finance at the University of California's Walter A. Haas School of Business and founder of Financial Engineering Associates (FEA), observes that FEA's emphasis has been on analytic VaR. Dr. Garman lists among the advantages of the analytic approach accuracy, simplicity, and limited computing demands. He believes that recent work on the VaR-delta technology may push the market back towards analytic VaR as VaR-delta is not obtainable via Monte Carlo. Another advantage, Dr. Garman adds, is that analytic VaR is capable of implementing real-time VaR trading limits whereas, he says, Monte Carlo is typically unsuitable for real-time use.

Figure 3.6
Numerical methods (on the right) correspond to the mathematical description of stochastic processes.

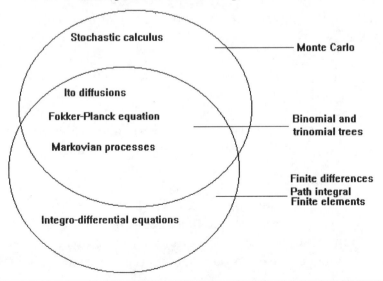

One of the limits of Monte Carlo methods, remarks Robert Selvaggio, head of the treasury analytics group at Chase Manhattan Bank, is that they are computer intensive and require special techniques for reducing the dimensionality of the path space. He adds that some products, such as callable debt, should be valued with backward-looking methods while Monte Carlo is forward-looking.

Efforts are under way to improve the efficiency of Monte Carlo algorithms. Farshid Jamshidian, managing director of product development and strategic trading at Sakura Global Capital in London, agrees that there are computational problems with conventional Monte Carlo approaches. He cites the need for a very large Monte Carlo sample to adequately capture all possible configurations of yield curves, exchange rates, and counterparty default scenarios. Still, simulation methods are needed to handle nonlinearities. Numerically sensible ways to do Monte Carlo are, Dr. Jamshidian says, required, especially for large portfolios.

To solve the problem of an excessive number of portfolio valuations, Jamshidian and Zhu (1997) developed a new approach to Monte Carlo, a scenario simulation model. The approach relies on factor analysis to understand the important factors that affect simulations. The advantages of this approach, according to Dr. Zhu, are: (1) it is efficient (runs on a workstation), (2) it can be used for real risk management, e.g., hedging books, (3) it allows to control how fat a tail one wants to see with more factors or scenarios, and (4) deltas, vegas, default risk, and country risk can be easily incorporated.

At Lehman Brothers, where Monte Carlo methods are considered important to their modeling effort, researchers are studying low-discrepancy sequences and methodologies to generate good paths. They are also working on convergence problems, a special path version used for a reducing the number of paths.

The New York-based consulting and software firm GAT uses the Linear Path Space (LPS) approach proposed by its founder Thomas Ho (1992), co-developer of the Ho-Lee interest-rate model. An intelligent sampling technique that speeds up Monte Carlo calculations, the LPS approach is based on creating equivalent classes of paths and then choosing a representative path from each class. The clustering criterion is whether the paths rise, fall, or remain unchanged within a specified period.

The use of adaptive computational methods for finding representative paths was frequently cited as a tool for reducing the computational complexity of simulation runs. Umberto Cherubini, head of forecasting and risk management research at the Milan-based Banca Commerciale Italiana, used Kohonen maps to cluster government bonds and then sample the clusters. A neural-network technology, Kohonen maps cluster events that can be represented by continuous variables.

References

Alexander, Carol, editor, *The Handbook of Risk Management and Analysis*, John Wiley & Sons, New York, NY 1996.

Alexander, Carol and C. Leigh, "On the Covariance Matrices Used in VaR Models," *Journal of Derivatives*, 4 no. 3: 50-62, 1997.

Artzner, Philippe, Freddy Delbaen, Jean-Marc Eber, and David Heath, "A Characterization of Measures of Risk," University Louis Pasteur, Institut de Recherche Mathématique Avancée, Strasbourg, France, February 1996.

Bassi, Franco, Paul Embrechts, and Maria Kafetzaki, "A Survival Kit on Quantile Estimation," Working Paper, Swiss Federal Institute of Technology-Zurich, Department of Mathematics, 1996.

Beder, Tanya Styblo, "VaR: Seductive but Dangerous," *Financial Analysts Journal*, September-October 1995.

Campbell, John Y., Andrew W. Lo, and A. Craig MacKinley, *The Econometrics of Financial Markets*, Princeton University Press, Princeton, NJ, 1997.

Dattatreya, Ravi E. and Frank J. Fabozzi, "The Risk Point Method for Measuring and Controlling Yield Curve Risk," *Financial Analysts Journal*, pp. 45-54, July-August 1995.

Embrechts, Paul, C. Klueppelberg, and T. Mikosch, *Modeling Extremal Events for Insurance and Finance*, Springer Verlag, 1997.

Fabozzi, Frank J. and H. Gifford Fong, *Advanced Fixed Income Portfolio Management*, Probus Publishing, Chicago, IL, 1994.

Ho, Thomas S.Y., "Managing Illiquid Bonds and the Linear Path Space," *The Journal of Fixed Income*, vol. 2, no. 1, June 1992.

Ho, Thomas S.Y., "Key Rate Durations: Measure of Interest Rate Risk," *The Journal of Fixed Income*, vol. 2, no. 2, September 1992.

Jamshidian, Farshid and Yu Zhu, "Scenario Simulation: Theory and Methodology," *Finance and Stochastics* 1(1), 43-67, January 1997.

Jarrow, Robert A. and Dilip B. Madan, "Arbitrage, Rational Bubbles, and Martingale Measures," Working Paper, Johnson Graduate School of Management, Cornell University, 1996.

Kleidon, Allan W., "Stock Market Crashes," Research Paper, no. 1262, Stanford University Graduate School of Business, January 1994.

Lawrence, Colin and Gary Robinson, "How Safe Is RiskMetrics?" *Risk Magazine*, vol. 8, no. 1, January 1995.

Lawrence, Colin, Gary Robinson, and Matthew Stiles, "Incorporating Liquidity into the Risk Measurement Framework," *Financial Derivatives and Risk Management*, June 1996.

Litterman, Robert, "Hot Spots and Hedges," *The Journal of Portfolio Management*, December 1996.

Reitano, Robert R., "Non-Parallel Yield Curve Shifts and Immunization," *Journal of Portfolio Management*, pp. 36-43, Spring 1992.

Zangari, Peter, "A VaR Methodology for Portfolios that Include Options," *RiskMetrics Monitor*, J.P. Morgan, New York, NY, First Quarter 1996.

Chapter 4

Credit Risk

4.1 MODELING CREDIT RISK

Credit risk is widely considered one of today's major challenges in risk management. There are modeling issues. There are pricing issues related to loans and to derivatives subject to credit risk. There is the problem of the integration of market and credit risk. Lastly, there is the question of the completion of the credit risk market through credit risk derivatives such as credit swaps.

For Robert Geske, vice president of C*ATS Software and professor of finance at the University of California-Los Angeles (UCLA), the biggest challenge in integrating market and credit risk is in the details and the available data. He remarks that because there is little agreement on the analysis of historical data in the area of credit risk, e.g., the default probabilities of AA or AAA-rated corporations, it is difficult to estimate, with a reasonable degree of certainty, default probabilities and credit transitions. An additional problem, Dr. Geske adds, is the lack of agreement on the proper measurement of credit risk.

Risk has been defined, in its generality, as uncertainty about the distribution of values around some expected value. For most securities, this concept applies to individual securities as well as to portfolios of securities. Credit risk is somewhat different. The default of a debtor is a sort of rare catastrophic event that can be described in probabilistic terms by the probability structure of its occurring and its severity.

Carol Alexander, University of Sussex researcher and academic director at the financial software firm Algorithmics, remarks that building good models for the credit derivatives market will be a major challenge. Modeling the distribution of expected losses in credit risk is, in fact, totally different from modeling market risk. The problem of credit risk, Dr. Alexander observes, is its skewness: it has a different shape than market risk and is non-normal for different reasons. It also has a different time horizon.

A critical issue related to representing default risk is the percentage that can be recovered in case of default, i.e., the severity of default. One problem in evaluating default severity is the representation of debt seniority. In case of default, debts are subject to priorities that are determined either by specific contractual agreements or by the law. Representing this structure in mathematical terms is not easy. In addition, as studies have shown, debt seniority is often violated.

Another challenge is the evaluation of change in the value of collateral. Collateral such as real-estate is subject to price fluctuations. Given the difficulty of modeling severity and of marking collateral to market value, modeling often assumes a fixed rate of recovery, i.e., a constant severity.

Assuming constant severity, one might use a Poisson process to model the default probability. More complex processes can be considered, for instance relating default probabilities to underlying economic variables such as interest rates. A different approach, originally proposed by Robert Merton, regards default as an option on the value of the firm.

The definition of credit risk could be broadened, considering not only the probability of default but also a parameter that expresses credit worthiness. This approach assigns a credit parameter, such as a credit rating, which is related to the value of the security under consideration.

Large listed firms are subject to rating by credit agencies. For these firms, credit risk is only marginally the probability of outright default; what is more relevant is the probability distribution of a change in rating. Such a change would affect the price of the firm's bonds and translate into market risk.

The determinants of credit risk can be summarized as shown in Figure 4.1: default probability, severity, and the probability of credit rating migration.

There are questions related to the empirical meaning of credit risk in the case of, say, AAA-rated firms. Meaning is given by the transition probabilities of the rating matrix, i.e., the probability that a firm's rating change. The system can be tested only at the periphery, when firms hit ratings that cause statistically meaningful failure rates.

Figure 4.1
Default probability, severity, and rating migration contribute to the credit risk measurement.

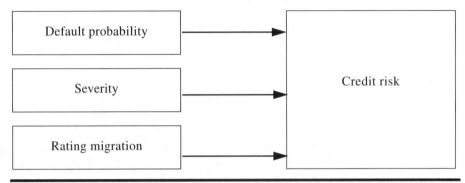

How can the default of a triple A-rated firm be modeled? Farshid Jamshidian of Sakura Global Capital remarks that they use stressed default probabilities. "Over short periods," he says, "it's a question of how conservative you want to be; for long periods, empirical probabilities may be more appropriate. There are conventional and judgemental elements." Noting that the stressed expected default rate of a triple-A firm is roughly 150 years, Dr. Jamshidian says there is a need to integrate judgement.

The above approaches model credit risk as a rare point event. When portfolios of securities are considered, however, credit risk becomes the actual distribution of portfolio values that the same portfolio might assume. Over sufficiently large portfolios and sufficiently long periods of time, credit ratings and default probabilities are measured by the statistical incidence of default events. This is the methodology for measuring credit risk adopted by J.P. Morgan in CreditMetrics. The same methodology can be applied in modeling credit risk related to lending to non-listed companies. These methodologies are particularly useful when adopting a financial approach to pricing and managing credit risk.

4.2 A PORTFOLIO APPROACH TO CREDIT RISK

The pricing of loans and the management of loan-related credit risk is now receiving a lot of attention. For John McQuown, a founding principal of software firm KMV, the major issue is corporate default risk. "It is," he says, "98% of the problem of risk today." Mr. McQuown notes that risk measurement is by and large new and that this applies "particularly, unambiguously" to default risk. The attitudes and processes in place in most institutions, he observes, implicitly assume that credit risk is subjective and cannot be measured.

Commenting on what's new in credit risk, Pierre Antolinez-Fehr, risk controller at Zuercher Kantonalbank, remarks that once based on a one-to-one relationship, credit risk is increasingly data-based and instruments for managing portfolios of credit risk are making their need felt. "We are moving," Mr. Antolinez-Fehr says, "towards a quantitative measurement of risk and the pricing of loans on a risk-adjusted basis."

A technology scenario for credit risk management consists of several steps. The first steps include the adoption of a portfolio approach to loans, the evaluation of default probabilities and correlations, and the identification of common default risk factors. Next, a pricing approach is developed. This requires, in the first instance, an actuarial approach to set a risk premium for default risk, but might extend to a no-arbitrage pricing approach that would allow the trading of credit derivatives.

The above scenario entails methods different from those now prevalent in credit assessment. Traditional credit assessment software typically attributes to each client a score that might be interpreted as a default probability. The classic procedure is to ask for and evaluate collateral and to grant loans equal to a fraction of the collateral's value if the score exceeds a certain threshold. In doing so, banks make close to risk-free loans though there may be costs related to liquidating collateral should this prove necessary.

A portfolio approach implies the evaluation of credit risk as joint probabilities of default over portfolios. In other words, it is important to assess not only the default probability of a firm but also the covariance of a firm's default with that of other firms in a portfolio. This approach is well known in equity portfolio management. The difficulty in the area of credit risk is due to the absence of traded securities that set prices.

A portfolio approach to credit risk has the beneficial effects of diversification and a corresponding reduction in risk. The principle of diversification is easily applied to portfolios of personal loans. These portfolios are close to being perfectly diversified and therefore nearly risk-free as there is little fluctuation around expected losses.

Portfolios of corporate credit, on the other hand, depend on common risk factors. These might be related to business sectors or to geographies. In fact, one of the major objectives of diversification is to protect against deterioration of the economy of a sector, a region, or a whole country. Understanding common risk factors is a question of factor analysis and econometric modeling.

There are substantial differences in the probability distribution of losses due to default in different portfolios. Large portfolios of personal loans are basically a default cost which is averaged over many different clients. The central-limit theorem applies; probability distributions reduce to highly peaked normal distributions.

Large portfolios of small-to-medium-sized enterprises (SMEs) are characterized by distributions that can be approximated by normal distributions. These portfolios are made up of different entities that, in aggregate, produce normal distributions. Though the probability of large losses is negligible, it is possible to optimize, pricing for clusters with different characteristics.

Lastly, portfolios of large enterprises with complex debt seniority structures show skewed distributions of returns, with small but not negligible probabilities of substantial losses. These debts are part of a financial structure that is partially traded in the market. Figure 4.2 shows the difference between the shape of return distributions of typical portfolios of market and credit risk.

Economic cycles add another dimension to the problem of estimating credit risk. Oeistein Garsjoemoen, deputy general manager in group risk management at Den norske Bank, cites large swings in the economy. Down two or three years ago, the Norwegian economy has now bounced back. Though the Oslo-based bank started collecting requisite data several years ago, Mr. Garsjoemoen remarks that good figures for long economic cycles are difficult to find. To calibrate the classification systems, better theories for long cycles are, he says, required.

Figure 4.2

The distribution of default losses in credit portfolios: comparison of the distribution of credit returns and market returns.

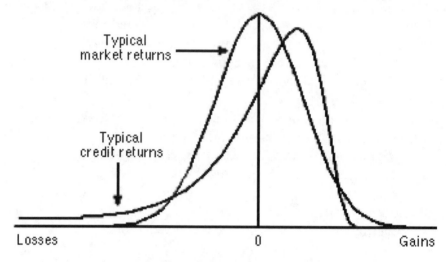

(Courtesy of J.P. MORGAN, CreditMetrics Technical Document.)

Academic research is beginning to tackle the problem of credit risk. An advocate of a portfolio approach to credit risk, Erasmus University Rotterdam professor of finance Ton Vorst notes the absence of a theory for evaluating and re-evaluating portfolios of loans. He suggests the adoption of models along the line of option pricing theory.

This opinion is shared by Alexander Wolfgring, head of risk management and ALCO support at Bank Austria. Mr. Wolfgring believes that the option theory might be used to integrate credit risk under the same concept as market risk. A positive side effect, he says, might be the ability to infer the right price even for non-listed companies. But Mr. Wolfgring cites the need to first change accounting policy as today's way of making provisions presents big discrepancies with the mark-to-market approach.

On the theory side, one of our interviewees cites the phenomenon of credit chains: money transactions are part of a chain of transactions; if one part breaks down, all else falls apart. The principle can be illustrated by the example of a home owner who wants to change homes. To buy a new home, he has to sell his present one, but his buyer gets laid off and all breaks down. There are market-wide effects. Credit risk is part of market frictions and, therefore, has an impact on the pricing of securities.

4.3 PRICING DERIVATIVES SUBJECT TO CREDIT RISK

The integration of credit risk in derivatives pricing requires mathematical models that fit the general no-arbitrage approach to bond and derivatives valuation. There are two major approaches. In the one, the basic risk determinant is a process that describes the evolution of a firm's value. Initially proposed by Robert Merton (1974) and subsequently extended, this approach views default as an option on the value of a firm; the option is exercised if the value falls below a certain threshold. Standard option-pricing techniques are used for pricing. Robert Geske (1977), of C*ATS Software in Los Angeles, applied this approach to price bonds subject to credit risk. Researchers, including David Shimko (1993), now at J.P. Morgan, and Naohiko Tejima and Donald van Deventer at The Kamakura Corporation extended Merton's approach.

A second approach represents credit risk as an external hazard process that causes default. Introduced by Robert Jarrow and Stuart Turnbull (1995), this approach initially assumed a constant recovery rate and a Poisson process for the hazard rate. The Jarrow-Turnbull approach has since been extended by Jarrow and Turnbull themselves, Darrell Duffie and Kenneth Singleton (1995) from Stanford, David Lando (1996) from the University of Copenhagen, and others to include more sophisticated processes for the recovery rate and the hazard process. Models of this type are called structural models.

It would be interesting to link default to macroeconomic parameters such as interest rates. This approach would be particularly fruitful with structural models, such as the one proposed by Jarrow and Turnbull, that consider default an external process. These models have been extended to take into account the correlations between default and interest rates.

Farshid Jamshidian of Sakura Global Capital believes that while it is theoretically possible to model joint movements of interest rates and defaults, the problem is too complex to be of practical use. Referring to efforts underway at Sakura, he remarks that the difficulty is in getting the data on correlations. Their scenario simulation model assumes no correlation between default incidents and interest rates. It utilizes the matrix of probability of change in rating provided by the rating agencies to generate joint (but independent) default and interest-rate scenarios.

4.4 MEASURING AND PRICING THE CREDIT RISK OF LISTED FIRMS

The financial approach to evaluating and pricing credit risk was pioneered by Oldrich Vasicek and subsequently implemented in the analytics developed by KMV Corporation (see Kealhofer, 1995 and McQuown, 1995), of which Dr. Vasicek was a founding partner. Robert Merton had shown how to use option theory to link the value of a firm to its underlying assets: default is an option on the value of the firm. The key insight is the ability to use the price of traded securities to estimate indirectly credit risk and correlations between credit risks. It also offers a scheme for credit risk pricing under the no-arbitrage framework.

As the no-arbitrage principle is assumed to hold for all securities, it is possible to infer non-observable credit-related parameters from the observation of the price of stocks, bonds, and their derivatives. The underlying reasoning is that the market, in its drive to exploit profit opportunities, is the best estimator of these parameters. Based on these principles, KMV developed analytics to estimate financial parameters such as rating migration probabilities and bond price correlations. These analytics were to provide many institutions, including J.P. Morgan, with the fundamental analytics for a portfolio approach to credit risk.

The KMV approach was incorporated into CreditMetrics, a generalized framework for credit risk measurement developed by J.P. Morgan and endorsed by a number of banks and KMV itself. Credit-

Metrics consists of a methodology and software that implements a portfolio approach to credit risk. It takes, as input, parameters such as credit rating migration probabilities and the time series of securities such as stocks and bonds. The output is a probability distribution of the credit returns and a measure of credit risk in a given portfolio.

These approaches project the matrix of transition probabilities of corporate ratings onto changes in the value of portfolios subject to those ratings. This enables the formulation of effective strategies for credit risk management even in cases where default is a rare phenomenon, e.g., the default of a triple A-rated firm. But this approach to credit risk can be used only with firms whose equities and debts are linked to market prices, allowing the application of the no-arbitrage principle. To evaluate and price the credit risk of non-listed firms, different techniques are required.

4.5 PRICING LOANS TO SMEs

While finance theory can be used to establish the credit rating of large listed firms, this is not the case for non-listed small-to-medium-sized enterprises (SMEs). Because the assets and liabilities of SMEs are not traded in the market, the no-arbitrage principle cannot be applied to the valuation of their credit risk. The default risk of SMEs is an independent source of uncertainty that adds a new risk dimension to the market. Pricing the credit risk of these firms requires the use of techniques for valuation in incomplete markets.

The starting point is the evaluation of default probabilities. Default probability distributions are generally nonlinear functions of default predictors such as corporate ratios. An innovative approach to this problem is the use of nonlinear methods such as Kohonen maps to segment borrowers into homogeneous classes for which default probabilities are statistically significant.

One source of methods for pricing loans to SMEs comes from the insurance sector, where actuarial methods are used to price insurance policies in function of the risk to cover. Actuarial methods fix the rules for the pricing of independent risks in function of risk attributes. They do so by establishing a meaningful relationship between risk measures and prices in the absence of a market that prices risk.

The application of actuarial methods to pricing loans to SMEs is not free from market considerations. The problem is to divide the cumulative premium that the lender wants to earn among the different risk classes in an optimal way, taking into account profitability and market share objectives.

4.6 CHALLENGES IN MANAGING CREDIT RISK

The methods used in credit risk management belong to a new set of methods that quantify risk previously outside the realm of quantitative measure. These methodologies include option pricing theory as well as behavioral modeling and factor analysis. They are used to value credit risk and non-maturity portfolios such as non-maturity deposits and credit card portfolios. The question of the mark-to-market value of non-maturity deposits was identified by KMV co-founder John McQuown as an important topic for resolution by commercial banks.

One bank that has made the switch to handling credit risk quantitatively on a portfolio basis is Barclays Bank. David Townsend, deputy director of the portfolio management unit at the London-based bank identifies three stages in credit risk: (1) the expected default frequency, (2) the volatility around the expectation of default, and (3) the joint default frequency, i.e., the correlation of default between companies. The latter is their area of concern. Grading models are used to calculate the expected loss which equals the expected default frequency (EDF) times the expected exposure on default times the severity:

Expected loss = expected default frequency
× expected exposure on default × severity.

The EDF part of the process requires econometric theory; the rest is based on data. KMV software is used in rating large corporations. For individuals and small-to-medium-sized enterprises

(SMEs), Barclays has created its own models which are updated as the data and the understanding of data improve.

Among the problems encountered, Mr. Townsend mentions the measurement of credit quality and that of joint default frequency. The latter cannot be observed historically and is considered a major problem at the moment. But by far the harder part of the whole problem, according to Mr. Townsend, is the database.

Measuring volatility is a problem when looking at non-listed firms. Dirk-Emma Baestaens, formerly professor of finance at Erasmus University Rotterdam and now head of R&D for credit at Generale Bank, remarks that this presents a problem to a bank such as theirs that deals with some 30,000 SMEs in Belgium. Because the only available data are corporate balance sheets, the Brussels-based bank uses implicit factor models. Option pricing is combined with information extracted from factor analysis.

Fluctuations in the value of collateral is another problem in credit risk management. Pierre Antolinez-Fehr, risk controller at the Swiss state-owned regional bank Zuercher Kantonalbank, says that their biggest risk — credit risk — has only recently been confronted with quantitative methods. Because the traditional way of dealing with credit risk is through calling collateral and pricing in function of the collateral, the main risk is real-estate risk.

Mr. Antolinez-Fehr cites the need for index-based derivatives to deal with fluctuations in property values, though establishing an index has met with difficulties. People dealing in real-estate, he remarks, are not familiar with the derivatives business, and there are theoretical problems. As such an index is not a traded security, there is not a sufficient number of securities to allow for replication. The bank has, nevertheless, prepared an index including some 9000 documented property sales. Regression-based, the index adjusts prices in function of market transactions.

In Norway, Den norske Bank is working on developing consistent principles for the pricing of loans. "We can't take the chance of not being able to price," says Eldbjoerg Sture, general manager in group risk management at the Oslo-based bank. "But how far we go with risk-based pricing will depend on our competitive position and what the rest of the market does." The bank wants to avoid volatility in pricing; the objective is to better understand the risk of each loan. Den norske Bank's clients include roughly half of all Norwegian businesses, from the small and medium-sized companies to large corporations.

The principles used in pricing at Den norske Bank are the same as those used in portfolio management: economic capital and expected loss through an economic cycle. Methods used to calibrate the pricing models are based on the RAROC principle for the largest corporations and econometrics and internally developed models for the SMEs. The common denominator is econometrics. Ms. Sture believes that a quantitative portfolio approach will grow in importance, despite the legal constraints of sharing data.

4.7 CREATING A MARKET FOR CREDIT RISK

Where are financial institutions in creating a market for credit risk? To diversify credit risk, the risk attributes of portfolios of loans must be traded, a capability that requires the development of a market for credit derivatives such as credit swaps. Most banks, in fact, expect to see the credit derivatives market develop, though perceptions on the timeframe vary.

Credit swaps have, until recently, remained inside financial firms. Zuercher Kantonalbank's Pierre Antolinez-Fehr cites several reasons. First, the information on which swap pricing is based is customer and bank specific, and information sharing is subject to legal restrictions. Second, because investment-grade customers rarely go bankrupt, taking probabilities of default is difficult and adjustment for it arbitrary.

The size of the market also plays a role. In Europe, Jean-François Boulier, head of risk management at CCF-Crédit Commercial de France, notes that up to now the market for credit derivatives has been too small to warrant its development. He believes, however, that the introduction of the European Monetary Union might change this. Jean-Marc Eber, head of R&D at Société Générale's capital markets department in Paris, notes that they are now witnessing a demand for credit risk models from their traders that was not there just two or three years ago.

In the UK, Barclays' David Townsend remarks that the high-street bank is moving towards loan trading, securitization, and credit derivatives. Mr. Townsend believes that, if one can short credit risk or diversify portfolios, the economics are sufficient to drive the market. He identifies as a major area of risk the consequences of serious deterioration in a regional or national economy and points to an index of credit worthiness of UK companies which should be in place sometime in 1997. The market for credit risk could, he thinks, be quite active shortly thereafter.

An idea of the potential size of the market for credit risk is given by John McQuown, a founding principal of KMV Corporation. Mr. McQuown notes that there are some 150 major firms that serve as points of origination of corporate debt and another 1000 to 3000 that serve as non-originating repositories. The total amount of outstanding corporate debt in OECD countries is equal to about 80% of all corporate equities or 80% of $10 trillion. This debt, which represents a large chunk of all economic activity in the OECD countries, is owned by not more than 5000 institutional investors. The key, Mr. McQuown says, is diversification. Debt cannot be hedged, but diversified portfolios can be constructed and traded. Mr. McQuown foresees a "monstrous" development of credit derivatives.

4.8 MODELING INSURANCE RISK

Paul Embrechts, professor of applied probability and insurance mathematics at the Swiss Federal Institute of Technology-Zurich, notes that an important convergence between banks and insurances firms is in act, not only at the business level where the two activities are being united, but also at the level of products. He cites the general area of the securitization of risk, credit insurance, and examples such as act-of-God bonds. It's a two-way exchange, Prof. Embrechts says, where both sides benefit: access to financial markets will give extra capacity to the insurance world while insurance-related products, such as credit insurance, RARORAC (risk-adjusted return on risk-adjusted capital) and solvency are areas where insurance can and does contribute new ideas. He also cites default risk as an area where more insurance thinking could be useful.

Prof. Embrechts believes that finance now has the tools required to move away, when necessary, from the technical assumptions underlying Black-Scholes and complete markets. The insurance world is, he notes, used to the concept of incompleteness and has done a lot of work with risk models in incomplete markets. Prof. Embrechts cites as an important research topic the comparison of actuarial and financial pricing. As banks converge to setting up strong risk management groups, he believes that actuarial training will be of growing importance for such groups.

There are, of course, differences between financial firms and insurance companies. One of these, according to Thomas Ho, co-developer of the Ho-Lee model and president of the consulting and software company GAT, is the time horizon. Dr. Ho remarks that while the time horizon of insurance companies is from 10 to 30 years, banks do short-term risk reporting, securities firms daily. "Whatever you do in banking or finance," Dr. Ho says "you need to know how reality can hit you in the short-term." In addition, he notes the different regulatory bodies and rules, different criteria for judging "prudence," and different organizational structures.

References

Aase, Knut and Bernt-Arne Oedegaard, "Empirical Tests of Models of Catastrophe Insurance Futures," Working Paper no. 96-18, The Wharton Financial Institutions Center, University of Pennsylvania, 1996.

Cherubini, Umberto and M. Esposito, "Options in and on Interest Rate Futures Contracts: Results From Martingale Pricing Theory," *Applied Mathematical Finance*, vol. 2, 1995.

Duffie, D. and K. Singleton, "Modeling Term Structure of Defaultable Bonds," Working Paper, Stanford University, 1995.

Embrechts, Paul, "Actuarial Versus Financial Pricing of Insurance," Working Paper no. 19-17, The Wharton Financial Institutions Center, University of Pennsylvania, 1996.

Geske, Robert, "The Valuation of Corporate Liabilities as Compound Options," *The Journal of Finance and Quantitative Analysis*, pp 541-552, 1977.

Jaffee, Dwight and Thomas Russell, "Catastrophe Insurance, Capital Markets and Uninsurable Risks," Working Paper no. 19-12, The Wharton Financial Institutions Center, University of Pennsylvania, 1996.

Jarrow, Robert A. and Stuart Turnbull, "Pricing Derivatives on Financial Securities Subject to Credit Risk," *The Journal of Finance*, vol. L, no. 1, March 1995.

Kealhofer, Stephen, "Portfolio Management of Default Risk," KMV Corporation, San Francisco, CA, 1995.

Lando, David, "Modelling Bonds and Derivatives with Default Risk," Working Paper, University of Copenhagen, Institute of Mathematical Statistics, February 1996.

McQuown, John A., "Market Versus Accounting Based Measures of Default Risk," KMV Corporation, San Francisco, CA, 1995.

Merton, Robert C., "On the Pricing of Corporate Debt: the Risk Structure of Interest Rates," *The Journal of Finance*, 2:449-470, May 1974.

Shimko, David, Naohiko Tejima, and Donald van Deventer, "The Pricing of Risky Debt When Interest Rates Are Stochastic," *The Journal of Fixed Income*, vol. 3, no. 2, September 1993.

Chapter 5

Managing Risk

5.1 THE RISK MANAGEMENT PROCESS

The management of risk is a process distinct from its measurement. It involves a set of institutional rules that are largely dependent on a firm's goals. Defining the rules is top management's job. The risk manager's job is to facilitate this process by providing an appropriate framework for decision making.

Harry Mendell, vice president with Morgan Stanley's market risk department, remarks that the key is to continually go back to the question "What is the goal of risk management?" If the goal is to produce reports required by the regulators, the process is one of engineering. But if the goal is wider, e.g., to optimize shareholder value, several dimensions of the problem come into play.

There is the perception that, with a few exceptions, the management of risk is a process poorly understood and only partially implemented. Looking at the industry as a whole, Philippe Buhannic, head of listed derivatives at Credit Suisse First Boston in New York, remarks that the risk management process is presently limited to giving figures to regulators and limits to traders. He observes that only a few banks are using historical data — without models — to allocate capital. The reasons, he says, are managerial and practical. At the managerial level, there is a lack of strong interest and traders are reluctant; at the practical level, it's a question of catching the data.

In Europe, Luc Henrard, head of risk management at Generale Bank, notes that relationship banking has been working against sound risk management. For Mr. Henrard, the challenge to European banks will be to change the culture at the top and to vastly improve the ability to collect data. As for the former, there is the requirement that members of the board become comfortable with statistical concepts such as confidence intervals and expected values. As for the latter, Mr. Henrard observes that in the past, data were collected for accounting needs. "A quantum leap must," he says, "be made, going from an ALM database to a risk management database."

The risk management process can be viewed as process control. In function of a firm's goals, the process starts with decisions on what risks to avoid or to eliminate through market mechanisms and what risks to manage actively. Elimination is achieved through hedging and/or diversification. The risk control process itself might be embodied in trading strategies that can be determined through mathematical algorithms or in the setting of limits, policies, and capital allocation (see Figure 5.1).

If risk can be controlled at the level of trading, mathematical optimization techniques can be employed to engineer trading strategies; there is a direct link between the measurement and the control of risk. If, however, it is not possible to control trading strategies, the principles involved are different; there are only indirect links between risk measurements and controlling actions.

When controlling risk indirectly, through policies, limits, and capital allocation, the risk factors are aggregate processes characterized by complex behavior. One might, for instance, impose limits on a trading desk. The actual process to be controlled, i.e., the trading of that specific desk, is difficult to formalize as it depends on the strategy of the trader. The link between controlling parameters such as limits and the behavior of aggregates such as trading desks or higher level aggregates is a poorly formalized process.

Figure 5.1

The risk management process.

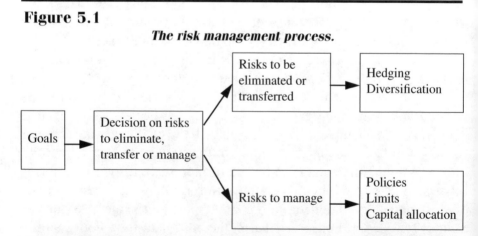

Formalizing the control of risk requires an understanding of — and eventually the modeling of — the behavior of traders and of risk aggregates that depend on the decision-making process. This might prove difficult. A trading desk does not behave as a simple security but shows complex behavior. By imposing limits, it might be possible to control the conditional risk over a given time horizon, but there might be hidden risks over other time horizons.

Thomas Ho, president of the consulting and software firm GAT, suggests viewing the risk management process as a manufacturing process with the quality assurance concept and a quality assurance manager responsible for the whole process. Unanticipated losses are the defects of the manufacturing process. The objective is to ensure a defect-free risk management process. Dr. Ho (1995) divides the process into five phases: (1) defining the requirements, e.g., target returns, risk tolerance, the investment benchmark, (2) the design phase which integrates economic research with the investment objective, (3) the test phase which includes the construction of a model portfolio and stress testing on it, (4) the implementation phase which involves buying and selling securities to implement portfolio strategies and performance evaluation, and (5) the maintenance phase which ensures that the investment cycle reflects the plan (see Figure 5.2).

Figure 5.2
The quality-based investment cycle proposed by GAT.

Design Phase:
Forecast market dynamics, adjust
for constraints, and set directions
for portfolio managers

Requirement Phase:
Monitor portfolio returns
and positions, and establish
goals to meet client's needs

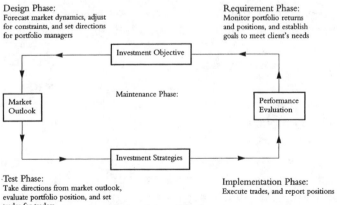

Maintenance Phase:

·Test Phase:
Take directions from market outlook,
evaluate portfolio position, and set
trades for traders

Implementation Phase:
Execute trades, and report positions

Source: Exhibit 1 in Thomas S.Y. Ho, "Quality-Based Instrument Cycle," *The Journal of Portfolio Management*, vol 22, no.1, Fall 1995, p. 64. This copyrighted material is reprinted from Institutional Investor, Inc., *The Journal of Portfolio Management*, 488 Madison Avenue, New York, NY 10022.

Yong Li, risk manager at Credit Lyonnais Americas, also draws a parallel from industry. The whole risk management process — identifying risk, measuring and monitoring it, and the strategic application of the process — requires a long time, Mr. Li says, before benefit can be derived. He points to the need to have a strategy to quickly realize benefits and suggests a prototyping approach comparable to that used in industrial design or manufacturing. The key, Mr. Li says, is to understand the specific corporate environment. He suggests starting with a careful study of the internal structure and building on this. "If not," he adds, "you find you spend lots of money to meet the objective and can't produce results to justify the costs."

5.2 THE TIME HORIZON OF RISK

The importance of the time horizon grows as risk management and ALM are brought under the same perspective, using similar approaches for handling various risks over different time horizons. For dealing room-based activities, the time horizon for risk management is generally defined as the period of time necessary to unwind positions. For ALM, the time horizon might be the period of time over which corporate results are evaluated. Investors might have even longer time horizons.

For Umberto Cherubini, head of forecasting and risk management research at Banca Commerciale Italiana, the time horizon for risk management is inherently short; though the same methodologies might be applied to ALM, the time horizon is different. "Confusing the two" he says "is like thinking about your future while crossing the street. If you don't pay attention to oncoming cars, you might not have any future to worry about." Behind this is the notion of risk management as a control function, ensuring that acceptable risk limits are not exceeded.

There are positions whose risk horizon is inherently long. Credit risk is an example. Credit worthiness changes relatively slowly over time; unwinding positions on commercial loans might take quite long or prove impossible. Market trends evolve over long periods, presenting long-term risks. Interviewees remarked that the difference in time horizons is a major problem in translating market and credit risk into a unified measure.

Carol Alexander, researcher in time-series analysis at the University of Sussex and academic director at the financial software firm Algorithmics, believes that credit derivatives are the solution to the time horizon problem, unifying market and credit risk under the same horizon. With the growing use of credit hedges, Dr. Alexander says, we will begin to focus on only short-term credit risk, as is already the case for market risk. The requirement: counterparties to develop a liquid market for credit risk.

In integrating different time horizons, the difficulty, as with many problems in financial modeling, is related to some basic short-coming in today's finance theory. At the heart of the problem is the lack of a tenable stochastic description of the economy that covers both details and long-term trends. To represent short-term risk, we use models that need continuous recalibration; when we take a long-term view, we ignore the short-term details.

Because stochastic representations are so approximate, we do not really know how risks compound in time. Short-term periods are condensed and conditional probability distributions evaluated at the end of each period. In managing risk, we assume that successive periods are basically independent from previous ones. For many risks, the assumption is reasonable; for others, involving long-term trends, it is not.

It is possible to stay within risk limits, e.g., VaR limits, for each period but still run risks over long periods given the correlations between subsequent periods. There might also be complex relationships between the short and long term. Credit and market risk are a case in point. Stochastic changes in credit worthiness are typically negligible over short periods but compound in time in different ways from market risk. Credit risk might be magnified through the use of derivatives. From the purely analytical point of view, market and credit risk can be integrated, but the continuous recalibration of models required makes their integration difficult in practice.

While it is technically possible to build an integrated framework for different types of risk, it is difficult to build an integrated framework for different types of risk and different time horizons. Models that span different periods of time must be built, making assumptions on the short and long-term behavior of risks.

Bernhard Hodler, co-head of global market risk management at Credit Suisse First Boston, observes that to integrate over a one-year period they measure risk over a 10-day unwinding period and scale up to one year after taking into account all possible time correlations. He notes that the parameters used for these calculations are not the same as those used in measuring short-term trading risk.

The problem of integrating different time horizons of risk is related to the problem of a global economic view of risk. The practice of risk management grew out of the need to control specific types of risk through financial engineering. As we move towards firmwide risk management and the integration of risk management and ALM, we begin to touch upon deeper economic questions.

There is presently the need to understand not only the fine details of complex contractual transactions but also the long-term risk factors. We saw this need in areas such as the modeling of loan default or prepayment behavior and the understanding of catastrophes. Risks such as these depend on structural properties of the economy and cannot be handled simply through contractual arrangements. Credit risk, for example, is a basic risk. It entails dissipation factors in the economy, as heat in physics. It can be diversified and, perhaps, hedged; this depends on fundamental properties of the economy.

Ultimately, the handling of different time horizons will require a more macroeconomic approach in risk management. This includes arriving at an understanding of basic risk factors, economic trends and structural changes, and of their compounding with complex contractual agreements such as derivatives. A shift from relative risks to true open risks is implied.

5.3 THE NOTION OF VALUE

In modern finance, value is related to market consensus: it is the price at which an asset is traded in the market. This is the essence of mark-to-market valuation schemes under which the value of a firm's assets and liabilities are "marked" to their current market value. Computing VaR is computing the change in the value of a portfolio of assets subsequent to changes in price.

This is a significant departure from the traditional methods of valuation and accrual in which assets have an intrinsic value and accruals make provision for possible deterioration of value. Within the traditional framework, values change over long, not short, periods. Through accruals and aggregation, large organizations can show quite arbitrary balance-sheet results for long periods of time. With mark-to-market valuation, the conventional side of balance-sheet measurement is significantly reduced as valuations of assets and liabilities reflect the current market value.

It is perhaps interesting to note that the financial notion of value differs from the macroeconomic notion of value. Macroeconomic theory posits that the economy produces an output which can be measured in real terms; only a scaling factor is undetermined. It assumes that it is possible to compare real outputs over different periods of time and eventually to compute an inflation factor.

The concept of price inflation is, however, extraneous to finance. The key concept of finance theory, the no-arbitrage principle, acts as the global coherent constraint for value. It does not, however, determine the global value of assets; these fluctuate in time. Equilibrium and optimality constraints, depending as they do on a characterization of agents that cannot be empirically ascertained, remain nearly arbitrary. As demonstrated by Jarrow and Madan (1996), finance theory is compatible with phenomenon such as speculative bubbles.

The no-arbitrage principle brings valuation under option theory. An important consequence of the no-arbitrage principle is the link between a firm's value and that of its assets. As stated by Robert Merton (1974), the value of a firm can be regarded as an option on the value of the firm's assets. Based on the no-arbitrage principle, option theory provides the theoretical link between the value of a firm and the value of its assets.

The no-arbitrage framework has other consequences. If a portfolio of assets can be replicated by another portfolio, both have the same value and will be undifferentiated by investors. In mathematical parlance, there will be a linear manifold of assets to which investors will be indifferent. This is the essence of the Modigliani-Miller theorem on the value of a firm which states that a firm's value is independent of its financial structure, e.g., shares versus debt financing.

A formidable consolidation of the notion of value, the no-arbitrage principle allows to understand and compare, under a single framework, the value of radically different categories of assets. It allows the valuation of assets that are not liquid; it allows a common treatment of different risks, such as market and credit risk. In other words, it allows to view valuation as the projection of the value of a limited number of factors.

As remarked by many interviewees, risk management is ultimately the optimization of shareholder value or the creation of added value for the shareholder. This concept is generally stated in terms of the hurdle rate or the average return in a given sector of business. Shareholder value is created by choosing investments that yield a return higher than the hurdle rate; it is destroyed by choosing investments that yield a return lower than the hurdle rate.

In reality, the question of shareholder value is quite complex. Under the no-arbitrage framework, and consequently under option theory, the relationship between optimum shareholder value and risk management policies can be made mathematically explicit, at least in principle. It implies, however, the explicit statement of the investors preferences in terms of risk.

5.4 THE RISK-RETURN RELATIONSHIP

Andre Shih, director of the software firm Treasury Services (Santa Monica, California), remarks that there is growing convergence between the notions of profitability and risk. He sees the market moving towards integrating the risk-return trade-off in summary measures, with risk moving towards those players that are most efficient at assuming it. Once concerned with minimizing risk, banks are now actively seeking risk. Money center banks, Mr. Shih observes, are going after markets and engineering structured-type transactions for institutions; on the retail side, banks are going from standard mortgages to products with more complex embedded options, such as deposits pricing linked to indices.

But while there is a conscious attempt on the part of financial firms to optimize the risk-return trade-off, a thorough mathematical understanding of the risk-return opportunities available in the market is lacking. In general, financial markets present a positive correlation between risk and return as higher expected returns are correlated with higher risks. A study by Jeremy Siegel (1997), professor of finance at the Wharton School of the University of Pennsylvania, showed that over the last fifty years, the average cumulative returns on USA and UK stocks were significantly higher that the corresponding returns on government bonds.

The essence is: risk is rewarded. The reward is set by market consensus. Investors require high returns to bear high risks with a nonlinear relationship that favors greater risk. As observed already by John Maynard Keynes, financial markets are well protected against risk and risk bearers generally make handsome profits in the long run, though they can occasionally suffer losses.

A thorough study of the risk-reward features of different markets is difficult to implement because the important risk-reward characterization of markets is related not only to individual securities, but to trading strategies. Understanding the risk-reward characteristics of a market implies a stochastic model of the economy as well as what is considered a measure of risk plus a model of the decision-making process of agents.

If individual securities are considered, there is yet no empirical proof that common measures of risk such as betas are positively correlated to expected returns (see Fama and French, 1992). This should not be surprising as agents optimize portfolios, not single securities.

The risk-reward characteristics of markets change in function of market sectors and time. In specific areas, the positive correlation of risk-return might be violated. Fred Stambaugh, global head of strategic risk management advisory at First Chicago NBD in London, observes that it is possible to earn big returns for taking little risk if one can find a customer niche and lay risk off in the secondary market. Mr. Stambaugh questions the simple formula that to earn a high return one must run a high risk. "The question," he says, "calls for careful investigation."

It would be interesting to arrive at a simple characterization of the risk-return profile of markets that might lead to strategies that can be implemented. Such a characterization has not been found. Taking simple measures of risk, it is not possible to ascertain the relationships between the risk and profit of a trading strategy in sound scientific terms.

In view of the above, is the notion of the remuneration of risk useful? The answer is a qualified yes. First, risk is remunerated for large aggregates where simple measures are meaningful. Taken over significant periods of time, stocks, for example, earn higher returns than bonds, as shown in Prof. Siegel's study. In addition, though there is no precise mathematical statement of the risk-return relationship, the relationship can be approximately ascertained for a number of markets.

The point is that it is possible to determine approximate relationships between risk and return, but it is not possible to refine the process. Ultimately, risk-return trade-offs in the most general situations are expressed through optimization algorithms that assume specific goal functions; assuming a simple positive correlation between risk and return might prove counterproductive. A thorough optimization analysis must be made before concluding that real risk-return opportunities are present.

5.5 DETERMINING THE RISK APPETITE

In theory, an organization determines its risk appetite and subsequently optimizes risk taking. Present finance theory describes this appetite with the utility function, a formal way of ordering risk preferences. In practice, however, organizations determine the types of risk they want to bear and the level of risk they consider optimal or acceptable with methods that are not formal.

Risk implies fluctuations in earnings and profits and, eventually, a small residual probability of bankruptcy. From the point of view of risk management theory, the type and amount of risk a firm wants to bear is a subjective management decision; it is a datum and cannot be substantiated theoretically.

Figure 5.3

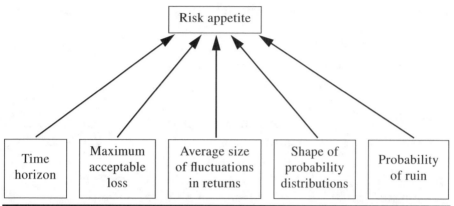

Parameters determining the risk appetite.

A number of parameters might structure the risk appetite of a firm. Among them are: (1) the time horizon over which risk is evaluated, (2) the maximum loss that a firm is willing to bear, (3) the average size of fluctuations in returns, typically represented by variance or VaR, (4) the shape of probability distributions, and (5) the residual probability of unrecoverable losses that a firm is willing to accept (see Figure 5.3). There might be other parameters for evaluating the risk appetite, e.g., strategic sectors or high-return lines of business.

It is fair to say that the process of deciding what risks to run is not well understood in a scientific sense. The above parameters are difficult to evaluate quantitatively and might imply different measurement schemes. From the behavioral point of view, risk taking is difficult to explain.

5.6 DIVERSIFICATION, HEDGING, AND PORTFOLIO MANAGEMENT

Viewing risk management as process control, the objectives of the exercise can be reflected in trading strategies to control or eliminate risk through diversification, hedging or, more in general, portfolio optimization. Conceptually speaking, diversification and hedging are both instances of the more general technique of stochastic optimization.

Diversification can be applied if risks are uncorrelated. Consider an investment with a given probability distribution of returns and, therefore, with a given expected return and a given risk. If there are a large number of similar uncorrelated investment opportunities, an investor can substantially reduce his or her risk by dividing his or her investment among uncorrelated investments. This is a mathematical consequence of the assumptions of independence and absence of correlation.

Financial investments cannot be perfectly diversified as there is always some correlation between risky investments. But by selecting a well diversified portfolio, risk can be substantially reduced. The residual risk depends on common factors affecting the distribution of returns. If one wants to eliminate or modify the risk left after diversification, i.e., the risk that depends on common risk factors, hedging is used.

Hedging involves investing in assets or portfolios whose risks offset each other. This means that there are investments whose probability distributions are perfectly anticorrelated, allowing to build risk-free portfolios. The most common technique for hedging is the use of sensitivity ratios (the Greeks) of derivatives prices with respect to the underlyings. By choosing portfolios in function of the Greeks, it is possible to make portfolios insensitive to some factor(s).

Hedging imposes a trade-off: to keep portfolios hedged, they must be continuously rebalanced, choosing appropriate combinations of Greeks that take into account second-order effects. But rebalancing does not come cheap: there are costs associated with transactions. The optimal trade-off between transaction costs and risk coverage must be determined.

A more radical approach to hedging uses scenario optimization, an instance of multistage optimization. The objective is not confined to local optimization but takes into consideration goals defined over all possible securities for the entire period. Intermediate optimizing decisions are taken into account upfront.

The ability to eliminate a specific risk does not imply that the economy is not exposed, globally, to that risk. It simply implies that there are other entities that are willing to bear that risk. If the economy is not exposed to a given risk globally because there are natural hedges, the price of that risk should be zero. This consideration suggests that, from the perspective of a financial firm, it is potentially highly rewarding to discover natural hedges due to the globalization of markets. Discovering these hedges involves identifying unexploited large-scale correlations and anticorrelations.

Diversification and hedging, as most operations in risk management, can be seen as an instance of portfolio optimization. In fact, portfolio optimization is historically the first application of risk management methods. Formal mathematical techniques are now applied to managing portfolios. Investors, or their managers, choose utility functions deemed fairly representative of their risk appetite. Portfolios are then selected with the aim of maximizing the expected value of utility over probability distributions of returns.

The technology of optimization has been extended to cover different investment management objectives. Pension funds might need to optimize investments in function of expected cashflows. Others might want to immunize portfolios against some specific factor(s). These problems can be cast in the framework of optimization, single-period or multistage. Diversification and hedging can be regarded as the outcome of multiperiod optimization processes.

Diversification, hedging, and, more generally, optimization are mathematical techniques for controlling risk. They can be used when one has the ability to control the trading strategies related to transactions or portfolios. At firmwide level, where the fine details of trading cannot be controlled, different risk control strategies are required.

5.7 POLICIES, LIMITS, AND CAPITAL ALLOCATION

Financial firms can be seen as a large array of decision-making processes that try, individually, to maximize profits by taking risks. Risk taking is inherent in decision making in finance: the higher the credit risk, the higher the premium; the more unique the forecast, the higher the potential reward. These single processes are optimizing processes, albeit informal. Controlling the fine details is not possible and perhaps not desirable. Clinton Lively, head of the global market risk group at Bankers Trust, observes that the business lines own the risk: uncertainty is so great that judgement must stay with those responsible for the business.

Managing risk on a global level is based on imposing limits and issuing guidelines. Limits express the way business is conducted and are a major tool in risk management. The risk manager puts up the hurdles, the business-line managers jump over. Senior management directs the business, raising or lowering the hurdles.

Colin Lawrence, head of global market risk at BZW Barclays in London, remarks that capital allocation and the setting of limits are among the most challenging aspects of risk management. At BZW, optimal capital allocation is linked to limits; their focus, Dr. Lawrence says, is here.

Much of the development in risk management systems has concentrated on ensuring that the flow of activities remains within agreed upon limits. Risk management systems monitor limits at various levels of aggregation. Current portfolio data are captured and run through models to measure the risk. But there is comparatively little methodology to assist management in the setting of limits and the allocation of resources. Though in principle optimization processes, their formalization has proved difficult. The accent is on business judgement.

The need to understand the business(es) the firm is in was frequently underlined by interviewees. Michael Winchell, senior managing director of risk management at Bear Stearns, describes management's task as follows:

- define acceptable loss limits determined by gradually demonstrated capabilities,
- understand the businesses under one's direction,
- limit the artifacts of settling losses (simple scenario analysis),
- set careful directives that are understood ("we don't want surprises" is not enough), and
- review regularly the sources of profit and loss.

The questions to ask, Mr. Winchell says are: How do we get into the positions we get into? Are we a volatility trader? A short options trader? Do we make money because our clients don't understand the securities they are buying? Because there are arbitrage conditions?

Mr. Winchell cites the need to focus on "inventory control," i.e., what one owns and what it is worth. Firms, he notes, can get caught up hiring mathematicians to understand what they are getting from their desks, but that is only part of the problem. Senior management must, Mr. Winchell says, spend time evaluating the firm's positions and communicating limits.

The optimization side of setting limits is reflected in the process of optimal capital allocation, i.e., resources should be placed where they yield the highest returns. But as return entails risk, resources should be placed where they yield the optimal risk-return trade-off. Some measure of risk and return is selected and the allocation of capital is optimized accordingly. This is the idea behind risk-adjusted return on capital (RAROC) introduced (and trade marked) by Bankers Trust. RAROC in its many versions has gained wide acceptance. Thomas Daula, a managing director in global risk management at Bankers Trust, remarks that RAROC provides a useful baseline; it is, he says, an understandable tool that helps to discipline the business.

In practice, just what measures of risk and return can be used for capital allocation is a subject of debate. VaR is a widely used measure of risk in capital allocation. But VaR does not capture the complete picture. Clinton Lively, senior managing director of global risk management at Bankers Trust, remarks that capital allocation requires not just a single measure of risk but a whole set of risk measures.

5.8 ALM

Once an accounting function that handled uncertainty through the mechanism of accruals, ALM is rapidly changing. The introduction of mark-to-market techniques has propelled the handling of uncertainty to first place, with the need to evaluate stochastically the fluctuations of a firm's balance sheet. This is leading to a convergence of methods between ALM and risk management.

Luc Henrard, head of risk management at Brussels-based Generale Bank, remarks that banks need to get away from the return-on-equity aspect: it doesn't work at all with large corporations because of the way they consolidate. Only cash and cash equivalents are relevant. Mr. Henrard cites the need for mark-to-market analysis and computing of economic capital.

Robert Selvaggio, head of the treasury analytics group at Chase Manhattan Bank, believes that a major development for commercial banks will be the overthrowing of the accrual accounting mentality for a shareholder value attitude. He sees the difference between ALM and risk management disappear as ALM is increasingly grounded in economic theory and arbitrage-free pricing processes. Dr. Selvaggio's group has the mandate to put the New York-based bank's entire balance sheet on VaR.

At Capital Market Risk Advisors, Tanya Styblo Beder remarks that as ALM and VaR come together, risk management is becoming everything but credit. But even credit departments, she observes, are beginning to apply the same techniques as market risk departments start to give their guidelines to credit management.

One might say that ALM is risk management with a balance-sheet time horizon. As banks move towards evaluating the stochastic distribution of balance-sheet results, selecting strategies that optimize profit in function of risk, new methodologies for understanding the balance sheet and new valuation methodologies for balance-sheet items are required.

Charles Richard, a founding principal of Chicago-based software firm Quantitative Risk Management (QRM), notes that among USA banks there is now little distinction between ALM, balance-sheet management, and risk management. "It's all part of one big process within the same framework," he says. "Though the focus is different, they all need the same set of sophisticated models. The pay-off is consistency of assumptions." The old-style ALM function will not disappear, he adds, but it will move up the technology ladder, using stochastic interest scenarios, running hundreds of scenarios as opposed to the several typical today.

The adoption of risk management methods in ALM presents challenges from the methodological point of view. The biggest of these is the integration of different types of risk under one single arbitrage-free framework.

Another problem is in the modeling. Chase Manhattan's Robert Selvaggio remarks that the major modeling challenges are outside purely rational behavior, e.g, prepayment on mortgages, demand deposits, credit-card portfolios. The latter, he says, is one of the most difficult problems to get a hold on. These problems imply econometrics and the modeling of consumer behavior. Hazard functions and pay down have to be estimated, looking at individual histories. Dr. Selvaggio believes that volatility forecasting is handled pretty well. The interesting and difficult problems, he remarks, are those where active liquid markets cannot be observed. This, he believes, calls for the use of largely econometric methods, e.g, in valuing deposits or credit risk.

David LaCross, CEO of Risk Management Technologies, observes that we are going towards a forward-looking VaR concept, typically using some form of Monte Carlo simulation for both valuation and forecasting (earnings at risk). "Risk management can not rely on the past repeating itself," he says, adding that institutions must recognize that their current risk profile can be altered significantly by future rate environments, institution strategy, and the customer response to both. Mr. LaCross advocates incorporating a variety of sub-models in the simulation process, handling phenomena such as prepayment behavior, credit losses, asset allocation, and funding and hedging strategies. "These sub-models," he says, "ensure that results remain internally consistent with any projected rate environment under consideration."

The need for better analytics for prepayment models was also cited by William Murray, principal of Trepp Risk Management in Boston. Mr. Murray notes that simulating a limited number of interest rate scenarios does not allow one to easily assign a probability distribution to the results. When simulating a wide range of interest rate scenarios, as with Monte Carlo simulations, it is necessary to integrate a prepayment model into the simulation process to ensure that the prepayment estimates are an appropriate function of the interest rate environment. "To conduct Monte Carlo simulation without a reliable prepayment model is," he says, "naive. It produces results that are of questionable value at best."

Figure 5.4

Building blocks for understanding uncertainty and valuing instruments.

The problem	The methodology
How to compute yield curves?	Yield-curve smoothing methodologies
How do rates evolve?	Term-structure models
How to manage default risk?	Credit-risk valuation models
How are cashflows affected by rates?	Prepayment and behavioral models
How do cashflows translate into values?	Valuation techniques
How robust are the results?	Stress testing

Referring to the need for more sophisticated techniques in ALM, Andre Shih, director at the software company Treasury Services, remarks that a large set of choices or building blocks are needed to understand uncertainty and value an instrument. His list of techniques for solving specific problems can be schematized as shown in Figure 5.4.

A number of interviewees advocated caution in introducing risk management methods to ALM. At Bank Austria, the risk manager reports for both classic ALM and risk trading positions. But Alexander Wolfgring, head of risk management and ALCO support at the Vienna-based bank, believes that there is the need to be prudent in introducing sophisticated mathematical techniques to bank books and credit risk. ALM managers have always considered the number applied to measuring risk a subjective number, he remarks, while with trading risk measurements there is the tendency to forget the subjectiveness behind the figures.

Another reason of caution among Europe's universal banks was cited by Generale Bank's head of risk management Luc Henrard. Commenting on the need to compute economic capital, Mr. Henrard advises caution in applying the risk management concept to capital allocation in wholesale banking. "Even if you compute risk per entity," he says, "you cannot adopt a stop-and-go approach to the business."

5.9 GLOBAL OPTIMIZATION

Among our interviewees, there is broad agreement that risk management is, in the end, an optimization function. At the firmwide level, the function is typically handled informally, without the use of optimization algorithms. At the trading level, there is a more widespread use of optimizers. Optimization is, however, destined to become a core technology in firmwide risk management.

There are numerous optimization techniques. In deterministic cases, optimization means finding the minima or maxima of some goal function subject to constraints. In this case, optimization is a rather well known technique with applications in every scientific and technological field.

Numerically speaking, optimization is handled through a number of mathematical programming techniques. Linear and quadratic programming are the best known examples. Important advances in the field of optimization include statistical techniques such as genetic algorithms and simulated annealing. Statistical optimization techniques, and in particular genetic algorithms, represent a new generation of effective and easy-to-use optimization tools. They allow the global optimization of problems formalized through a goal function that has many minima or maxima. These techniques avoid getting stuck in local optima, a problem typical of standard mathematical programming methods.

Optimization methods can be extended to cover non-deterministic cases. One might want to find the optimal solution to a problem expressed in probabilistic terms. These problems are translated into deterministic maximization problems by choosing appropriate utility functions. If probability distributions are known, the expected value of utility functions is maximized. This approach is typical in portfolio optimization.

Stochastic optimization becomes tricky in considering multiple periods. In this case, optimization rules must take into account, at every stage, that decisions may be revised at each future stage. The process then becomes one of multistage stochastic optimization. Appendix A.5.1 introduces some of the principal concepts of stochastic optimization, including the notion of the deterministic equivalent of a stochastic optimization problem.

The use of multistage stochastic optimization techniques in finance is quite recent. The algorithms are complex, the techniques difficult to apply. They require large amounts of data for statistical estimates and are computationally intensive. Multistage stochastic optimization holds, however, the promise of significant advances in the risk management process; unlike other optimization techniques which are only local, multistage optimization offers the possibility of controlling risk on a global basis.

Industry take-up of optimizers, such as the multistage stochastic ones, has been uneven to date. Andrew Morton, co-developer of the Heath-Jarrow-Morton interest-rate model and now at Lehman Brothers, remarks that this class of problems is not confronted in the derivatives business due to limitations in computing power. Their focus, he says, is fair pricing with local hedges. In fixed income, Michael Chen, research associate at software and consulting firm GAT, remarks that they focus on the delta/gamma method. He observes that one can optimize only for single portfolios: it is still too difficult to tackle the bigger picture.

John Hull, co-developer of the Hull-White interest-rate model and co-founder of Toronto-based A-J Financial Systems, sees a role, albeit limited, for optimization in risk management. Risk management, he says, has the task of answering the questions "What is the risk?" and "Is it acceptable?" If the risk is not acceptable, a decision has to be made and this is where, according to Dr. Hull, optimization comes in. He cites the need for senior managers and regulators to understand the risk measurement methodology and suggests that there is a trend towards less use of the Greeks.

Some firms are, however, moving in the direction of optimizing information coming out of the risk management system. This is the case at Sakura Global Capital according to Yu Zhu, head of risk assessment and control in New York. But in looking at the industry as a whole, Dr. Zhu notes that financial firms are not experienced in loss management. Huge efforts have been made to build risk management systems and, while Dr. Zhu foresees risk management for resource allocation, he observes that its use is, for the moment, limited.

Some of our interviewees identified technical problems. For Tanya Styblo Beder, principal of Capital Market Risk Advisors, today's mathematics is too weak for optimization. The markets have too much emotion and mapping is a big problem. Jean Dermine, professor of banking and finance at INSEAD, adds what he considers obstacles to global optimization: the lack of data and of stable correlations between different lines of business. Today, he says, capital allocation is done on an ad hoc basis; correlations between credit and interest rate risk rely on intuition.

Multistage stochastic optimization might, nevertheless, turn risk management problems into robust algorithmic methodologies. Every risk management problem can, in fact, be cast in the framework of an optimization problem. This includes applications from hedging to portfolio immunization.

Toronto-based Algorithmics offers a suite of multistage stochastic optimization applications based on the work of its founder Ron Dembo. Formerly a professor on the management and computer science faculties at Yale University, Dr. Dembo developed scenario optimization as a generalized approach to financial optimization. This approach can be used instead of the Greeks to determine optimal hedges. Because it optimizes over multiple periods, scenario optimization has the advantage of creating hedges that are not local. Assuming the ability to describe scenarios, the same technology could be applied at the firmwide level.

The scenario optimization algorithms developed by Dr. Dembo are contained in Algorithmics' flagship product RiskWatch. If a problem can be described by a set of scenarios, RiskWatch can find an optimal solution.

Dr. Dembo believes that a new paradigm, with stochastic optimization at its pinnacle, is emerging. He sees the world as populated by players with different views on scenarios. The objective of the players is to minimize capital at risk over a given period, i.e., their regret function. It is this regret function that drives the players.

5.10 AGGREGATING RISKS

Effectively managing risk requires a global view of risks at many levels. The aggregation of risks might change the overall picture, revealing previously hidden correlations. Integrating different risks might have leverage effects or lead to diversification and hedging.

But aggregating and integrating different types of risk is not a straightforward task. At the trading level, it must be understood if traders are hedging each other's positions, effectively reducing the global risk. New York-based software supplier GAT is working on a formal approach to solving this problem, building in correlations of risk between desks in function of the business line. GAT's president Thomas Ho remarks that the real challenge is the modeling of business behavior and the organization chart.

Another problem of aggregation appears when integrating different types of risk related to the same securities. An example is the integration of market and credit risk, a very clear trend today.

A problem encountered in translating market and credit risk into one uniform measure or system is the difference in time horizons. A one-day holding period for the trading activity does not make much sense in commercial credit risk. Another problem is related to distribution assumptions: those made about the market do not fit with credit data.

As we move towards an integrated view of risk, Andre Shih, director at Treasury Services, notes that, despite the difficulties, there is convergence in looking at both market and credit risk on a single-number basis. He cites work being done by Robert Jarrow at Cornell University on valuation. Prof. Jarrow takes the principles of finance, and in particular option pricing theory, and applies them to credit risk. The goal of Jarrow's work is to produce a benchmark that can tell where the value line is.

5.11 THE ORGANIZATION AND INFORMATION FLOWS

Large risk management failures make headlines regularly. Thomas Ho, president of the consulting and software firm GAT, remarks that the key questions behind these failures are "What went wrong?" and "How can it be avoided?" Given the large personal stakes in the business, Dr. Ho adds that these are not trivial questions. Relying on personal ethics and standards of behavior is a rather weak proposition. There is a need, he says, to understand the mechanics of trading and the implementation of controls strong enough to avoid problems but allowing for profits.

Interviewees shared a high degree of sensitivity to the importance of organizational issues and communication flows in risk management. In one sense, this is obvious. What is less obvious is how to design an organization and the communication flows that serve the needs of risk management.

Andrew Morton, head of the fixed-income derivatives analytics group at Lehman Brothers, puts the accent on communication. Communication, i.e., expressing risk in terms that everyone understands is, he believes, the key issue in aggregation for firmwide risk management. Dr. Morton identifies three steps in the process: (1) the definition of a common description of risk, (2) an understanding of how the risk limits of individual businesses affect the risk limits of other businesses, and (3) going from aggregation to correlations. "Estimating correlations is dicey," Dr. Morton says. "There is the danger that people are correlating simple numbers that all break down."

At J.P. Morgan, a report on daily earnings at risk (DEaR) is produced at 4:15 and presented to senior management that same day, Monday through Friday. The report, subsequently dubbed the 4:15 report, includes the DEaR and VaR numbers as a total plus components. Risks are investigated down to the level of the trading desk. The 4:15 report is just one method in the firm's global risk management system, says Peter Zangari, vice president of risk management research at J.P. Morgan.

At Bankers Trust, where a centralized risk management group dates back to 1987/88, global risk collected from some 170 profit centers is measured and reported to management daily. On a weekly basis, the risk management group provides an overview of portfolio risk and significant exposures to the firm's management committee. "We all sit around a table," Clinton Lively, head of the global market risk group, says, "and review the weekly risk summary." Specific items such as individual trades, details on portfolios, trend lines, driving factors, potential liquidity, and credit risk are listed, and next to each risk is the name of person who runs the risk. "The objective," Mr. Lively adds, "is to ensure full transparency of risk and confirm that our risk profile is consistent with our market view and business strategy."

Effective risk management implies a balance of power between the risk manager and the persons he or she is supposed to control. Richard Klotz, partner in charge of global risk management at Coopers & Lybrand, remarks that institutions generally don't blow up because they don't do stress testing or good VaR, but because the risk management group either does not exist or lacks the authority to enforce limits or act if limits are violated.

There is, however, the need to avoid antagonism. Tension between traders and risk management can result if traders feel that risk management is too conservative. Jessica James, a member of the strategic risk management group at First Chicago NBD in London, suggests communication and information to solve the problem.

Colin Lawrence, head of global market risk at BZW Barclays in London, remarks that confrontation between the risk manager and traders often comes from organizations where standards were lax. The solution: emphasize the optimality side of risk management, helping traders achieve their goals. "Take them on the selfish side," he says.

5.12 THE MARKET FOR RISK

Risk management is based on the ability to buy and sell risk in the market. This means that, by investing in appropriate portfolios or by modifying the composition of existing portfolios, it is possible to choose any probability distribution of cashflows. The process of engineering risk can be implemented at every level of risk aggregation, from the portfolio level to the firmwide level.

The ability to buy and sell risk has been vastly improved with the stripping of risk attributes through the creation of derivative securities. Investors — if able to do correct analyses — can modify the risk profiles of their portfolios with a reasonable degree of accuracy.

One might ask why it is possible to offload risk onto other parties, i.e., why there are hedging opportunities. The first consideration is that there are movements that offset each other naturally. An increase in the price of oil is a gain for the oil companies but is a loss for the airlines and vice versa. The two parties might make an agreement to smooth over the fluctuations in their positions. This is the essential of natural hedges, i.e., of investments that are anticorrelated for some underlying economic reason. But hedging can also reflect the desire of investors to increase expected returns by taking a risk.

Is it always possible to find the desired risk attributes or the desired investment? Markets are said to be complete if it is possible to create portfolios that implement arbitrary probability distributions of cashflows or, in other words, if it is always possible to find investments with the desired return distributions. Given a complete market, every new cashflow stream can be priced by arbitrage arguments. In fact, any stream of cashflows can be replicated by a trading strategy, thus generating a risk-free portfolio. Market completeness depends on the interplay between objective risks in the economy and the availability of appropriate traded securities.

Many interviewees consider market completeness a key issue. Completing markets will be important to explaining the market price of risk and the time factor, and to increasing the dimension of the financial structure of the market.

In fact, real markets are not perfectly complete but show gaps in the ability to implement distributions of cashflows. An important practical question is how to complete markets. In intuitive terms, markets can be completed if, given any risk, it is possible to find a pool of investors willing and able to cover the risk. There are technical and economic problems in completing markets.

On the technical side, it is a question of engineering contracts with the desired properties. Derivatives play an important role in completing markets. The characteristics of the cashflows specified by derivative contracts are responsible for their probability distribution. On the economic side, it is a question of there being investors willing to take both sides of a position. Pricing, economic driving forces, and different economic views come into play.

Ron Dembo, founder of software firm Algorithmics, comments that if everyone does delta hedging — and most people do — all go out to buy futures at the same time, making it more difficult to hedge. But, he adds, even if the major financial firms use the same techniques, they will still hedge each other's risks as they have slightly different views. This leads to greater liquidity. Michael Zerbs, head of financial engineering at Algorithmics, notes that as financial products become more and more mathematical, it is possible to meet specific hedging needs better.

In incomplete markets, prices are not set by the no-arbitrage condition. In fact, securities introduced to incomplete markets cannot be replicated by existing securities. This poses problems of valuation:

derivatives become primary securities and therefore genuinely risky, i.e., they cannot be hedged. Investors that take on these risks must have economic reasons for doing so and the ability to cover the risks.

New schemes for completing markets are being proposed. There is presently a push to take to the market credit risk or risks traditionally covered by insurance companies. Whether these schemes will prove viable or not is essentially the question of whether markets can be completed.

Robert Jarrow, professor of investment management at Cornell University's Johnson Graduate School of Management, remarks that market completion is a continuum. How far one can go depends on what one's holding fixed and what one can vary as an individual, a corporation, a country, or the world. "You can stabilize wealth to recession as an individual," Prof. Jarrow says, "but what if everybody wants to do the same thing? If the entire system swells together, you have a problem."

Thomas Ho, president of GAT, notes that USA capital markets are so free that it is possible to sell just about anything. He observes that over the last five years there has been considerable growth in the area of intermediaries that sell high-return risk to those willing to buy it. "The list of matchable risk is moving," Dr. Ho says.

In the credit risk market, David Townsend, deputy director of Barclays' portfolio management unit, believes that there is ample room for diversification trades in the area of credit risk. He cites work done on geographical diversification with historical data: results showed that 30% of the volatility was taken out of the market working with just the OECD countries.

According to Mr. Townsend, one factor that has been holding back the development of credit swaps and derivatives is the relatively high spread on trades, which, he says, will have to be reduced to one or two basis points as in other swap markets. He foresees the development of a separate set of investors who buy and sell credit risk, with the banks acting as intermediaries, developing new products and managing credit risk for others.

One might ask how risk management techniques will affect the global risk present in the economy. Some, including Ron Dembo and Michael Zerbs at Algorithmics, do not believe that risk management systems will reduce volatility. Dr. Zerbs comments that the implementation of value-at-risk limits may actually magnify volatility shocks in the market as rising volatilities force financial institutions to liquidate or hedge positions to reduce their value at risk. As the trading volume increases, he adds, volatilities may go up further, starting a vicious circle that could result in greater overall volatility.

Yu Zhu, director of risk assessment and control at Sakura Capital Markets in New York, notes that volatility is related to the global economic cycle and technology. It is not clear, Dr. Zhu says, that risk management will reduce macroeconomic volatility.

References

Amihud, Yakov, Bent Jesper Christensen, and Haim Mendelson, "Further Evidence on the Risk-Return Relationship," Research Paper no. 1248, Stanford University Graduate School of Business, November 1992.

Bekaert, Geert, Robert J. Hodrick, and David A. Marshall, "The Implications of First-Order Risk Averson for Asset Market Risk Premiums," Research Paper no. 1286, Stanford University Graduate School of Business, January 1994.

Dembo, Ron S., "Scenario Optimization," *Annals of Operations Research*, vol. 30, 1991.

Dembo, Ron S. and Alan J. King, "Tracking Models and the Optimal Regret Distribution in Asset Allocation," *Applied Stochastic Models and Data Analysis*, vol. 8, 1992.

Dembo, Ron S., "Scenario Immunization," Chapter 12, *Financial Optimization*, editor S.A. Zenios, Cambridge University Press, Cambridge, 1993.

Fama, Eugene F. and Kenneth R. French, "The Cross-section of Expected Stock Returns," *The Journal of Finance*, 47:427-465, 1992.

Ho, Thomas S.Y., "Quality-Based Investment Cycle," *The Journal of Portfolio Management*, vol. 22, no. 1, Fall 1995.

Jarrow, Robert A. and Dilip B. Madan, "Arbitrage, Rational Bubbles, and Martingale Measures," Working Paper, Johnson Graduate School of Management, Cornell University, 1996.

Merton, Robert C., "On the Pricing of Corporate Debt: the Risk Structure of Interest Rates," *Journal of Finance*, 2:449-470, May 1974.

Santomero, Anthony M., "Commercial Bank Risk Management: An Analysis of the Process," Working Paper 95-11, The Wharton Financial Institutions Center, University of Pennsylvania, 1995.

Siegel, Jeremy J., "Risk and Returns: Start with the Building Blocks," *Financial Times Mastering Finance* 1, London, 12 May 1997.

Chapter 6

Issues

6.1 DATA

The modeling of derivatives has occupied the forefront in the discussion on risk management, largely because it is based on sophisticated mathematics that imply an upgrade in the core competence of staff in financial firms and, in particular, of treasury staff in banks. But data are universally perceived to be a major issue in risk management. David LaCross, CEO of the software firm Risk Management Technologies, remarks that to go beyond the trading room, with an objective of firmwide risk management, there is a need for efficient access to the universe of transaction data held in an institution. He cites recent advances in hardware and software technology as an enabler.

Risk measurement methodology is based on two components, market constraints and the description of fundamental risk determinants. Market constraints reflect the laws of finance. Relatively well understood, the mathematics of constraints is based on how contracts are written and on general characteristics of financial markets, namely the no-arbitrage principle. The crucial point is to understand the real risk present in the economy, the evolution of basic risk determinants, and their relation to other economic variables. At every stage in modeling, we are confronted with the problem of evaluating parameters and analyzing the factors of risk.

Data requirements differ from business to business. Data are not a primary concern in the derivatives business, a high-tech market driven by contract specifications. Andrew Morton, head of the analytics group in fixed-income derivatives at Lehman Brothers, observes that in derivatives modeling only a small number of inputs are required to value a product. But in fixed income, he adds, where getting good price quotes on bonds can be difficult, data are a problem. Dr. Morton remarks that big data sets are also required for indexed products.

123

A different angle to the problem of data was cited by Luc Henrard, head of risk management at Brussels-based Generale Bank. Looking forward to the introduction of the Euro, Mr. Henrard remarks, "There is simply no historical data."

The problem of data is particularly acute in credit risk management. Balance-sheet data of non-listed companies can be unreliable or insufficient for purposes of analysis; pertinent transaction data is frequently either not in the computer or not stored for more than one year. Data available to a single bank might be statistically insufficient. Dirk-Emma Baestaens, head of R&D for central credit at Generale Bank, remarks that to exploit the default correlation structure, one needs a massive number — tens of thousands — of loan originations.

KMV Corporation, a San Francisco-based firm that develops methods for default risk measurement and management, is tackling the problem by encouraging data sharing. But many banks are hesitant as data are perceived to be a competitive advantage. Generale Bank's Luc Henrard observes that there is a reluctance among continental banks to compare or share data to pilot a more statistically significant database, even when identifying information is omitted. Barclays' deputy director of portfolio management David Townsend believes that the situation might change if banks come to believe that sharing data will lead to better decisions.

In some countries, such as Norway, the data problem is less of a constraint than elsewhere. Oeistein Garsjoemoen, deputy general manager in group risk management at Den norske Bank, remarks that good data — government or commercial — is available on listed and non-listed companies alike.

Another issue is data integration. "It is," says Keith Bear, head of risk management at IBM Europe, "the big issue. It is where 80% of the money is being spent." When projects are stalled, he adds, more often than not it is due to the complex problem of data integration. QRM's founding principal Charles Richard cautions, nevertheless, against what he calls "data paralysis."

Risk Management Technologies' David LaCross observes that a key prerequisite for firmwide decision support is to capture legacy-system data in normalized data repositories. The data repository is an essential first step towards organizing and optimizing data for use by analytical applications.

New intelligent technologies might help reduce the severity of the problem of data integration. Walter Taylor, securities industry director at Digital Equipment Corporation, believes that firms will find a way to use the data they have with intelligent programs that automatically search data, put them into different formats, take the fields that they need, and feed them into models to produce the desired results.

Data also present conceptual problems as raw data must be turned into secondary (i.e., derived) variables through preprocessing algorithms, often a key part of the process. The data-mining process can be decomposed into three steps: (1) gathering raw data, (2) building secondary variables based on raw data, and (3) factor analysis to identify key variables.

John McQuown, co-founder of KMV Corporation, underlines the problem of data on the price of corporate debt exposures. Unlike in the equity markets where prices can be observed, the prices at which corporate debt exposure changes hands in the secondary markets are hidden from the view by dealers and regulators. Data must therefore be reconstructed, using theoretical considerations such as option theory.

Yu Zhu, head of risk assessment and control at Sakura Global Capital in New York, points to the time window for analyzing data. Exponential weighting is fine for one-day risk analysis, he says, but puts too much emphasis on recent data. On the other hand, the relevancy of data more than one year old is often questionable. Increasingly required by the regulators, "conventional" data might, Dr. Zhu adds, be the best one can get.

The problem of conventional data is typical in science. In the physical sciences, most data are obtained through a measurement process that is theory-laden. Temperature, for instance, is measured through the readings of instruments that make use of the full body of thermodynamic theory, linking temperature with other physical quantities. The measurement of temperature, even as an idealization, is performed through derived properties. As finance progresses in the direction of science, it will make increasing use of data that depend on finance theory itself.

The importance of data analysis is reflected in the amount of computing power devoted to the task. Major Wall Street firms have purchased large parallel machines for analyzing data. According to Harry Mendell at Morgan Stanley, data analysis absorbs more than half of their computational resources, more than modeling. "As we delve deeper and deeper into the data," Mr. Mendell says, "thirst for computing will be endless." A future objective: analyzing securities individually. Doing so for some 10,000 stocks in real time using multifactor models is not yet possible.

6.2 INTEGRATING PROCESSES AND METHODOLOGIES

Integration is a ubiquitous concern in computer-based methodologies today. "People are only now realizing what a big problem this is," remarks Carol Alexander at the University of Sussex. "It is," she adds, "a major focus today. Every time a new piece of software is introduced, a new interface is needed." According to Dr. Alexander, it's not just a question of nuts-and-bolts, but encompasses the vertical and horizontal integration of data and methodologies. Vertical integration must deal with the problem that different software, e.g., front and back office programs, might use different sets of theoretical assumptions and mathematics; horizontal integration must deal with the need to net different exposures worldwide.

Challenges related to integrating the different types of risk were mentioned in previous chapters. In the absence of an all-encompassing long-term stochastic description of the economy, the integration of market and credit risk remains conceptually problematic. Solving difficulties related to the integration of different time horizons confronted when the risk management and ALM functions converge is of growing importance as we move towards risk management as global optimization implicit in the notion of creating shareholder value.

The problem of integrating different areas of data, i.e., abundant data for "business as usual" but only scarce data for extreme events, is particularly tricky as fat tails must be taken into account. Though more effective statistical tools for handling extreme events are now available, it is still necessary to distinguish between areas where statistics can be applied and areas where no probability statements can be made. In the former, statistics can be used to price and allocate resources; the latter calls for other techniques. Integrating the two is a question of exercising judgement.

The various summary measures of risk currently in use pose additional integration problems. Each measure is partial and serves some specific purpose. The total risk picture cannot be summarized in one single number without losing information. Integrating the different risk measures is again a question of judgement.

The need to integrate business judgement also stems from the uncertainties and approximations inherent in the risk measurement process and the subjective elements inherent in the risk management process. Clinton Lively, senior managing director of global risk management at Bankers Trust, remarks that uncertainty is so great — not only in the probabilistic sense but also as regards the entire mathematical process — that judgement is essential. It is not simply the notion that, because measurements are only approximate, judgement must be exercised. Judgemental integration means that measurements offer only partial views that need to be integrated in a coherent decision-making process.

If a firm does optimization, the CEO owns the businesses and allocates resources. What is the information required to perform optimization mathematically? How far can the automation of the risk management process be taken? There are two facets to the latter question: 1) establishing decision rules and 2) the automation of the process itself. While everyone agrees that establishing rules is the domain of top management, there are differences of opinion as to the extent to which the decision-making process can be automated.

6.3 CLARITY OF COMMUNICATION AND CREDIBILITY

The firm's attitude towards risk must be clearly defined, communicated, understood, and shared throughout the organization. Clarity of communication, credibility and consistency emerge as fundamental determinants of sound risk management.

Paul Embrechts, professor of applied probability and insurance mathematics at the Swiss Federal Institute of Technology-Zurich and a co-founder of Risklab, notes that by asking at all organizational levels questions such as "How is risk defined?" "How is information provided?" and "How much risk are we prepared to bear?" financial firms and regulators alike are giving the importance of communication inside firms a shove.

The need for transparency and a fair playing field was emphasized by Colin Lawrence, head of global market risk at BZW Barclays. For Dr. Lawrence, a cascading structure of information with identification of profit and loss at every level is key. He adds the requirement that the board, management, and traders all share the same ideas about risk and strategy. As for the process, Dr. Lawrence advocates proximity, with a risk manager in every business on the floor. "Physical contact," he says, "is crucial. Technology can't replace it. Even if you have real-time information, you don't know what's in the trader's mind."

The importance of clarity of communication is reflected in the need for a common language for describing risk. As one of our interviewees notes, everyone uses a different language for describing risk: in the derivatives business, it's the Greeks, in equities the betas, etc. "People," he says, "should learn to talk *to* each other rather than *away from* each other."

At Société Generale, the problem is being tackled at the level of formal languages. The capital markets division's R&D group headed by Jean-Marc Eber is developing a language for describing financial products and interpreters for the language. The project includes work on semantic models of financial description languages. The goal: to have a quantitative and qualitative description of positions in the system.

6.4 THE SKILL SET

The risk a firm runs depends, ultimately, on the people running the firm. The importance of people — from ethical conduct to skills — was frequently raised. This does not mean that risk management should rely on trust, a weak proposition, as remarked by GAT president Thomas Ho, given the large personal stakes involved. For a number of our interviewees, the ability of a firm to manage risk is determined by both the quality of the people and the structure that the firm puts up. The need for people equally qualified, ranked, and independent in all areas of the business, from trading to credit and risk management control, was cited together with a clear separation of duties.

Commenting on the skill set, in particular of traders, Martin Dooney, head of global money markets at BZW Barclays, remarks that the information overload is pushing up the requisite for both academic qualification and emotional stability. A Bachelor of Arts or equivalent is, he says, no longer sufficient. BZW puts recruits through an initial three months of training. "It's bottom-line driven," Mr. Dooney comments. "The objective is to reduce the number of recruits that don't make it and to optimize the performance of those that do."

Mr. Dooney underlines the importance of analyzing traders' behavior, an area where they have been working now for a couple of years. Traders, he notes, often make mistakes due to untimely information or misinterpretation of data. What's important, he says, is to determine early on genuine errors and to detect deterioration in a trader's performance. Already working with the UK's DERA (Defense Evaluation & Research Agency) on a visualization application, Mr. Dooney remarks that the military also has performance evaluation technology for testing behavior under stress that could be of interest.

In New York, the question of training financial risk management practitioners and researchers was addressed by the recent formation of GARP (Global Association of Risk Professionals). A not-for-profit association of over 1,000 risk professionals, GARP provides a certification program for persons working in financial risk management and related fields. Yong Li, with Credit Lyonnais Americas' independent risk oversight unit and director of GARP's risk management education program, remarks that a successful risk manager is a "doer, an implementer," with a comprehensive set of skills. Among the requisite skills, Mr. Li lists an understanding of financial markets, economic and financial analytic ability, and a knowledge of computing technology. Comparing the risk management process to the quality control process, he underlines the need to build up components and skill sets internally, with more than just short-term goals.

6.5 REGULATORS

John Hull, professor of finance at the University of Toronto and co-developer of the Hull-White interest-rate model, remarks that regulators have played a critical role in raising industry awareness of risk. "They are influencing even the big players who like to stay ahead of regulations," he says. This is the consensus of our interviewees, at least as far as market risk is concerned.

Tanya Styblo Beder, principal of Capital Market Risk Advisors, notes that what regulators are trying to do is force a minimum standard of prudence. They are, she says, after some type of risk calculation that incorporates important variables. While the Bank for International Settlements (BIS) focuses on VaR, Ms. Beder believes that regulators also have a good grasp of the fact that no single calculation is right.

Regulators are also playing an active role in pursuing credit risk management with the banks, albeit a role very different from that played in market risk management. On the market side, the publicity given to big losses pushed the regulators to move, speeding up the introduction of risk management methodologies. On the credit side, Zuercher Kantonalbank's Pierre Antolinez-Fehr notes, there have been no such high-profile losses, despite the substantial credit losses over the past few years. The objective of the regulators has been to limit the risk, not to push the optimization of risk-return. That, Mr. Antolinez-Fehr says, is the bank's job.

6.6 PERFORMANCE MEASUREMENT

Risk management being the resource optimization task of a bank, it is reasonable to ask how well each business line performs. Unfortunately, measuring risk management performance is not simple, not even conceptually.

Conceptually, performance measurement compares an ex-ante decision-making process with ex-post realized gains or losses. Ex-ante decision making is based on forecasts and optimization processes. Whatever techniques one might use, from hunch and intuition to sophisticated forecasting and optimization algorithms, he or she is confronted with the problem of selecting a sequence of investments under uncertainty.

How can we measure ex post how well either task was performed? As regards the accuracy of forecasts, one has to assume that the actual history reveals the probability structure at the moment decisions were made. This implies assuming that one can judge the quality of the forecasts made, comparing the probability distributions that were used in the forecasts with the actual historical distribution of returns. This is far from being an obvious process when time-dependent probability distributions are used.

The ex-ante decision-making process might be a conceptually complex process that takes into account the risk appetite of the firm. There are a number of management decisions at the frontier of rare events that might be considered sound regardless of what actually happened. Optimization algorithms might use complex objective functions; the resultant decisions cannot be reduced to a simple ex-post evaluation.

A complex decision-making process under uncertainty requires performance measurements of similar complexity as it takes into account even remote and logically complex contingencies. From a practical standpoint, however, what is needed is a simple measurement process; investors want to see the pay-off. The subtleties of sophisticated decision making is of interest only to those that actually manage assets.

To simplify the task of performance measurement, only relative performance is considered. In other words, conventional benchmarks are established and results compared to those of the benchmark. Risk-adjusted performance measurements are based on this principle. A simple measure of risk is chosen, in general the variance of returns, results are adjusted in function of this measure and compared to some benchmark.

There are obvious pitfalls in this approach. Simple measures of risk are often inadequate. Historical distributions might not correspond to theoretical probability distributions. Periods under consideration might be too short to show all contingencies. Consider, for instance, a scheme of betting against interest rates. One might show above-average performance with little or no risk for a long time; the actual risk might have been much higher.

Performance measurements are somewhat conventional. There is nothing wrong with this, but choosing a performance measurement is not an insignificant part of managing risk. Management will typically try to optimize performance and, therefore, to implement a risk management scheme that optimizes in function of the selected performance measurements.

As risk management consists in making decisions about future contingencies under uncertainty, it entails a considerable and uneliminable level of arbitrariness. We are not able to translate probability judgements into time statistics with a reasonable level of scientific accuracy: samples are too small and the rules change with time. The subjective element is large. While tools assist in performing risk management optimization in scientific ways, the key decisions are management's.

In the long run, the market rewards risk taking. How much risk to take is a subjective decision; attempting to capture the complexities of this process with a simple performance measurement is clearly an oversimplification.

Chapter 7

Looking Ahead

7.1 THE CHALLENGES

As the focus of risk management shifts from a control function to one of global financial optimization, the concern shifts from modeling the behavior of engineered contracts (i.e., derivatives) in selected markets to modeling the evolution of the entire economy. This change of focus calls for a vastly improved ability to model the time evolution of economic quantities.

José Scheinkman, Alvin H. Baum professor of economics at the University of Chicago, remarks that, while those who do risk management are interested in predicting if assets will go up or down, the over-riding interest is in the relationship in movement of different assets. Though linear methods such as variance-covariance help to understand the co-movements of markets, a different set of tools is, Prof. Scheinkman says, necessary to better manage risk. Among these tools, he cites more efficient Monte Carlo simulations, learning, nonlinear dynamics, and statistical mechanics. Once the realm of academic research, these tools are moving closer to industrial implementation.

Paradigms such as learning, nonlinear dynamics and statistical mechanics will affect how risk — from market and credit risk to operations risk — is managed. While the first attempts to use some of these tools were focused on predicting market movements, it is now clear that these methodologies might shed light on many other aspects of economics. They could, for instance, be useful in understanding phenomena such as price formation, the emergence of bankruptcy chains, or patterns of boom-and-bust cycles.

Lars Hansen, Homer J. Livingston professor of economics at the University of Chicago, remarks that these new paradigms will bring to asset pricing and risk management an enhanced understanding once the implicit underlying fundamentals are better understood. "What is needed," he says, "is a formal specification of the market structure, the microeconomic uncertainty, and the investor preferences that is consistent with the posited nonlinear models." Commenting on the need to bring together the pricing of financial assets and the real economy, Prof. Hansen notes that an understanding of what's behind pricing leads to a better understanding of how assets behave. "For risk management decisions that entail long-run commitments," he observes, "it is particularly important to understand, beyond a purely statistical model, what is governing the underlying movements in security prices."

Blake LeBaron, professor of economics at the University of Wisconsin-Madison, observes that there is now more interest in macro moves than in individual markets. But traditional macroeconomics typically provides only point forecasts of macro aggregates. In the risk management context, Prof. LeBaron remarks, a simple point forecast is not sufficient; a complete validated probabilistic framework is needed to perform operations such as hedging or optimization. "One is," he says, "after an entire statistical decision-making process. The big issue is the distinction between forecasts and decisions."

Arriving at an entire statistical decision-making process implies reaching a better scientific explanation of economic reality. New theories are attempting to do so through models that reflect empirical data more faithfully than traditional models. By improving the description of the time evolution of specific financial markets or of the economy as a whole, these models will improve our ability to forecast economic and financial phenomena.

The endeavor is not without its challenges. Our ability to model the evolution of the economy is limited. Prof. Scheinkman notes that unlike in a physical system where better data and more computing power can lead to better predictions, in social systems when a new level of understanding is gained, agents start to use new methods, thereby changing the "laws of motion." Such systems, of which the economy is an example, are called self-referential.

One might argue that self-referentiality is a question of the "level" of laws; at the appropriate level, laws should be able to describe agent learning as well as the impact of learning on the environment to be described. In the economy, however, many obstacles stand in the way of comprehensive modeling: phenomena are complex and experiments cannot be performed.

"Less ambitious goals," Prof. Scheinkman says, "have to be set." Gaining an understanding of the broad features of how the structure of an economic system evolves or of relationships between parts of the system might be all that can be achieved. Prof. Scheinkman remarks that we might have to concentrate on finding those patterns of economic behavior that are not destroyed, at least not in the short-run, by the agent learning process.

The time scale of our knowledge is also important. Our ability to write laws that describe the economy depends on the interplay between the coarse graining of information and how far into the future we want to look. As the economy might be driven by nonlinear dynamics, as for instance is the case with weather, our predictive ability might be limited to the near or very near-term future.

This chapter explores the development of new paradigms of scientific explanation in economics. It starts by looking at developments that will be changing the way risk is measured and managed in the coming years. The focus is on new models outside the neoclassical framework and the increasing automation of the risk management process. The chapter then examines research efforts whose impact — potentially considerable — will take longer to work its way into industry. In particular, it will look at the paradigms of learning, nonlinear dynamics, and statistical mechanics.

7.2 THE NEXT FEW YEARS

Risk management models examined in previous chapters implicitly assume that agents are price-takers. A fundamental pillar of neoclassical finance theory, the postulate of agents as price-takers is, however, clearly violated in many situations of relevance to risk management. Trading, in particular, cannot be modeled with an acceptable degree of accuracy without taking into account the effect of trades on pricing, the most important component of the cost of trades.

The diffusion of program trading — a technique by which large blocks or baskets of securities are traded in a single transaction — has brought the problem to the forefront. To ensure the profitability of a trade, predictions on how the sale or purchase of large blocks of securities might affect their price would be useful. This requires the modeling of trading.

Market microstructure theory is tackling the problem of price formation at the trading level. Different conceptual schemes have been proposed. One line of thinking assumes monopolistic traders and an order-flow process. Price formation is derived as the inventory equilibrium condition of traders. A different theoretical approach is derived from game theory, with prices emerging from the interplay of agents with different levels of information. See Appendix A.7.1 for an introduction to these and other approaches.

An approach with practical implications for securities trading was introduced recently by BARRA (Berkeley, California) with the Market Impact Model. Based on an internally developed theory of market impact which assumes that trades disturb equilibrium, the model forecasts the cost (market impact plus brokerage commissions) incurred in stock transactions.

Nicolo Torre, manager of special products at BARRA, says that they take the view that when a market participant places an order, he or she purchases liquidity. They then ask what the risks are that the counterparty bears to buy the risk, analyze the risk, and price it. The novelty of the approach is that it models dynamically changing stochastic environments and asks how the system sets to a new equilibrium after perturbation. The time horizon is in the order of hours.

BARRA's theory is based on five factors: elasticity, volume distribution, volatility, trading intensity, and market tone. Elasticity measures the sensitivity of the order flow to price changes; volatility is price volatility; trading intensity is the speed at which orders arrive; the trade size is the average size of individual trades, i.e., trading volume divided by the number of trades for a given period, for example, one day; market tone is the market price of risk. A theoretical model links these factors for different types of markets and trading conditions; parameters were estimated through empirical research, using nonlinear maximum likelihood techniques.

BARRA Market Impact Models are risk management models in that they deal with uncertainty related to trading. Using the models, a trader can estimate the risk-return profile of a possible trade and decide ex ante the optimal trading strategy.

Models such as BARRA's mark a departure from classical risk management models: they model the market as a system to which one can apply stimuli and obtain a response. It is possible to foresee a new generation of models working as input/output systems in many situations. Changes in interest rates, for instance, typically produce a shift of investments between stocks and fixed income assets. Modeling this behavior as an input/output system (Figure 7.1) might prove fruitful.

There is the need to understand how to put together channels of the economy. Prof. LeBaron suggests that we might want to reconsider methods that look at interconnections, such as Leontieff's input/output tables. But the downside of such an approach, he adds, is that economies (i.e., what is produced, where and how) change so quickly.

Dr. Torre compares the risk management process to a portfolio management process: models receive as input information on returns, risks, and costs and calculate the optimized outcome. The problem, Dr. Torre notes, is one of developing the correct inputs. At the level of portfolio management, a number of firms have already completely automated the investment decision-making process. Trading and risk management will be progressively pulled into the process.

Technology is the enabling factor. Commenting on what he sees of interest happening in risk management, Prof. Scheinkman notes two parallel developments. On one side, trades are getting larger and the liquidity in markets is increasing. On the other side, computer power is cheapening, our understanding of financial assets improving, and algorithms are getting better. The former is leading to increased risks; the latter is making better risk management possible.

Figure 7.1

The market as an input/output system.

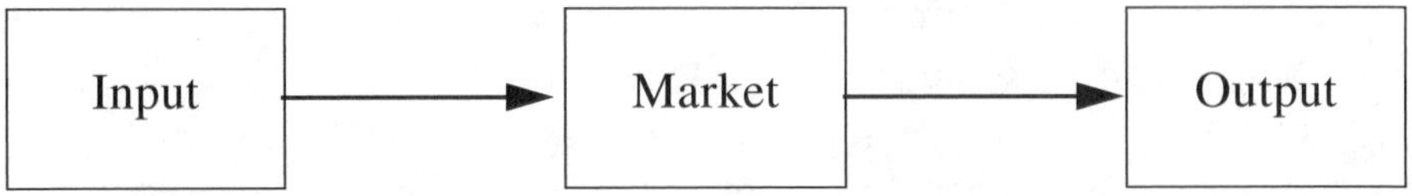

Given this scenario, Prof. Scheinkman observes, firms are now able to install real-time risk management tools, including the real-time computation of VaR and volatility, to compute and change their portfolios. "We will see firms doing risk management with a lot of tasks automated," he remarks. "At every trade, the trader will know the risk cost of the trade that will be charged to him."

Prof. LeBaron believes that we are not far from a solution to a fully automated statistical decision-making process in some markets. The problem, he notes, is one of converting forecasts into action, understanding what goes into the procedure and how the procedure feeds back into the forecast. Working in the area of technical trading rules at MIT's Center for Biological & Computational Learning, Prof. LeBaron believes that a solution is within sight for the simple case, e.g., trading in specific markets. He notes, however, that a firmwide statistical decision-making process, though not completely intractable, is much farther off.

7.3 SCIENTIFIC RELATIVISM AND THEORY CHOICE

Milton Friedman is credited with having first observed that economic theories should not be judged on how realistic their assumptions are, but on how well they explain empirical facts. By the standards of today's physical sciences, this observation is quite obvious. Theories are judged not on how reasonable they seem, but on how well they fit experimental data. Modern theories of physics might seem highly "unreasonable," yet they fit experimental data with an amazing degree of accuracy.

The question of theory choice, however, is more subtle and articulate than this seems to suggest. Modern science takes for granted that theories fit data and focuses on the deeper questions of theory verification, interpretation, and reduction. The question of verification is related to scientific relativism: no finite set of observations can conclusively prove or disprove any theory. Interpretation is the question of whether and how theories describe a "true" reality or whether they are just "recipes" for predicting the results of experiments. Reduction is the question of inferring a theory from more basic theories.

As economics becomes more of a science — thanks also to the availability of vast amounts of data — these questions become critical. We will start by exploring verification; interpretation and reduction, in particular with reference to rational expectations, will be explored subsequently.

The question of empirical verification affects all sciences. It can be stated — somewhat crudely — as follows: no finite set of observations can conclusively prove or disprove a theory. There is an infinite set of possible theories that are compatible with any set of finite observations; a theory can always be adjusted to fit experimental data.

Worse, just what an observation is is questionable. In the jargon of the philosophy of science, empirical observations are *theory laden*: what we take as basic empirical observations are not "pure" facts but facts interpreted through theory. Likewise, any measurement is the result of a process interpreted through theory; a risk measure means different things under different probability schemes.

The basic problem of empirical science — the inability of proving or disproving a theory on a finite set of observations — was first stated by the British philosopher David Hume in the eighteenth century. It has been discussed ever since. In this century, many solutions — some quite radical as, for instance, logical positivism — have been advanced. There is now agreement that the problem raised by Hume cannot be solved at a theoretical level. In other words, there is agreement that no finite set of empirical observations can conclusively settle any scientific question.

Opinions vary as to how to cope, both in theory and practice, with this fundamental limitation. Bertrand Russell and, presently, Willard van Orman Quine are the champions of a line of thought that maintains that science is a hypothetical logical construction that impinges on experiments *in toto* and only at the periphery. As adjustments within a theory are always possible, it is the entire theory, not single statements, that has to pass the empirical test. This is now mainstream in the philosophy of science.

Different theories might explain the same data within different conceptual frameworks. How does science choose among competing theories? Empirical accuracy is an all-important criterion for the adoption or rejection of theories. But observations being theory laden, empirical accuracy might be a somewhat conventional criterion. Consider risk: the meaning of accuracy as regards risk measurements depends on the framework one is working under. The adoption of a new theory is often a question of mathematical convenience and "aesthetics." The history of science offers many examples of this process; relativity is one such.

The above considerations lead to scientific relativism and pragmatism. Scientific relativism took an important bent with the works of Thomas Kuhn (1970) and Paul Feyerabend (1975). Kuhn first, and later Feyerabend in a more extreme fashion, observed that the adoption of theories is dictated by social, political, and economic pressure. Economics is particularly subject to this phenomenon.

University of Wisconsin-Madison professors William Brock and Steven Durlauf (1997) developed a formal model of theory choice in science. Their model takes into account both scientific and social criteria for the adoption of models and theories. Building on their earlier work on the dynamics of discrete choices in multiagent systems, they show formally the dynamics of the process of theory choice, modeling phenomena such as consensus aggregation. Consensus aggregation, they conclude, is not necessarily an obstacle to change; it may actually force change.

The importance of this model is twofold: it formalizes the dynamics of the process of scientific discovery under the constraints of social interaction and might be applied to economics itself. In particular, the model might shed light on the choice/rejection of rational expectations models. It might also serve as a building block for addressing the problem of self-referentiality of learning in economics (see 7.8 below for a discussion on self-referentiality and rational expectations).

It is appropriate to ask how science, and physics in particular, copes with the problem of scientific relativism given the amazing apparent success of scientific endeavors. Scientists are pragmatic, at least in their professional activity. Since the advent of quantum mechanics and the analysis of the *school of Copenhagen* led by the physicist Niels Bohr in the 1930s, science is seen (essentially) as an endeavor to build models, i.e., as recipes to predict the outcome of experiments.

Scientists are content if models correctly predict the outcome of experiments *within the present conceptual scheme of science*. In other words, experiments are observations that can be described within the scientific framework. The framework itself is conceptually stratified. Quantum mechanics, for instance, requires classical mechanics to describe observations.

Many consider this situation conceptually unsatisfactory and are trying to build an interpretation of science that might be considered descriptive of reality. This effort is problematic. Whatever image of reality can be built starting from today's science, it is certainly far from any intuitive notion of reality.

It is widely believed that *any phenomenon that can be described in the physical sciences* can be explained, at least in principle, with the present set of laws. This might change, but today's physical sciences are quite complete within the realm of applicability. Qualifications must be made as there are domains still outside of today's physical sciences. Cosmology offers one set of unresolved conceptual questions, the self-referentiality of human consciousness another.

In physics, we have a set of models, not entirely unified and not entirely coherent, but able to explain and predict, at least in principle, any set of observations that can be described within its language and conceptual framework. There is, however, neither agreement on the interpretation of the model, nor on whether models are "true," nor even if the latter question is meaningful. Nevertheless, when tested, these models make predictions that show an amazing degree of correspondence with experiments; no experiment is known to require a major revision.

7.4 THE EMPIRICAL CONTENT OF ECONOMIC THEORIES

In economics, the ability of models to predict the outcome of experiments (i.e., observations) is less satisfactory than in physics. We have, to start with, a number of empirical observations. Some of them are quite primary (e.g., bid/ask quotes); others are questionable and theory-laden (e.g., measures of GNP or inflation). Inflation measurements, for instance, depend on some primary theory of real economic growth which is far from being universally accepted. In addition, experiments cannot be performed; we have to settle for "experiments" that the economy performs for us, i.e., the actual course of events.

Present general equilibrium theories are problematic: they are general to the point of being untestable. Hansen and Heckman (1996) observe that there are different ways to make this claim. They cite, for instance, Harrison and Kreps (1979) who showed that a competitive equilibrium can always be constructed to rationalize an arbitrage-free dividend-price process. They suggest two possible attitudes in response to this state of affairs. One is to consider this indeterminacy as valuable flexibility that allows to understand very basic phenomena. The other is to simply dismiss general equilibrium models as empirically irrelevant.

To avoid the latter, of scant scientific interest, Hansen and Heckman propose to enrich, and eventually modify, the theory of general equilibrium. Analyzing proposals to constrain and estimate or calibrate various parameters in the general equilibrium models, they show how these are only ad hoc methods to force a match between theory and observation.

Hansen and Heckman suggest that the solution is to increase both the empirical and the modeling content of economic theory, taking into account and explaining theoretically micro data such as the structure of agent aggregation. In the process, one might discover the need to revise the general equilibrium paradigm and define a more comprehensive theory that can be reduced to general equilibrium models under special situations.

To enrich economic theory is to find models that better fit actual data in a meaningful way, i.e., without the indeterminacy that comes from arbitrary functions or terms left unspecified by the theory. It might also imply the introduction of a broader set of observables that enrich the empirical content of theories.

This might happen at different levels. The BARRA Market Impact Model introduces a number of aggregate variables that describe the market. The model — and this is the key point — places these variables in a theoretical framework and meaningfully connects them to empirical observations. Other models might consider variables at a more detailed level, for instance at the individual agent level, but the basic principle is the same: theory and observations are linked.

Meaningless in isolation, observables acquire meaning when they become part of a global theoretical framework. This is the essence of the statement that theories confront experiments in toto. Science seeks the most parsimonious explanation possible, i.e., it builds mathematical models with a minimal number of variables. At an early stage of scientific development, it might prove necessary to introduce new independent observables. At a later stage, the same observables might become terms that the theory is successful in predicting.

In the case of physics, it took hundreds of years to identify the present minimal set of variables. In the last century, thermodynamics added new quantities including heat, temperature, and entropy. Through the development of statistical mechanics at the beginning of this century, these quantities were subsequently reduced to more fundamental mechanical quantities. In the last fifty years, new variables including exotic ones such as "charm" and "color" have been added to describe the most elementary particles. The process is on-going.

At the present stage of development, economic theory is still searching for an appropriate descriptive framework that is empirically and theoretically meaningful. Alan Kirman, professor of economics at the Institute of Social Sciences (EHESS) and the University of Aix-Marseille, observes that the few summary variables presently used in macroeconomics are probably insufficient; other variables that take into account the structure of phenomena should, he remarks, be considered.

7.5 TESTING ECONOMIC THEORIES

Assuming that sufficiently rich explanatory theories can be constructed, the problem remains one of linking theories with observations. Theories are not tested in the abstract. Testing a theory implies developing a set of mathematical inferences that identify specific testable facts implied by the theory to be tested.

The difficulty of theory testing in economics is due to the fact that we typically work with statistical estimates of processes of which only one realization is known. Probability estimates can therefore be performed only through time statistics. In its most accomplished mathematical formulation, economic theory is expressed in the language of continuous-time stochastic processes. How can these processes be empirically tested?

In the physical sciences, the problem is less severe: there is an abundance of data, experiments can be engineered and observations replicated under identical conditions. Though physical laws are generally expressed in continuous-time mathematics, it is typically possible to select experimental settings that allow a careful evaluation of parameters. Yet a number of experimental findings are due essentially to the ability to derive appropriately testable mathematical implications. Particle physics is a case in point: often experimental evidence is obtained only through complex mathematical deductions.

In economics, a well established body of knowledge exists on learning and statistical estimates for processes that can be easily discretized. But statistical estimates related to continuous-time processes are much less studied. Only recently have methods been proposed for estimating parameters for continuous-time Markov processes. Among these are a set of new methods for estimating parameters of nonlinear Markov processes proposed by the University of Chicago professors Lars Hansen and José Scheinkman. Their methodologies are based on the representation of Markov processes through the associated infinitesimal generators.

Infinitesimal generators are operators that can be associated to each continuous-time Markov process. It is possible to show that there is a correspondence between the stochastic differential equations generally used in finance theory and deterministic differential equations that involve the associated infinitesimal generators. There are well known examples of the latter in statistical mechanics, for instance the Kolmogorov or Fokker-Planck equations associated to diffusions.

Hansen and Scheinkman (1995, 1997) showed how to estimate and test Markov processes from a discrete and finite set of data sampled from the same processes using the mathematical technology of infinitesimal generators. The mathematics is complex but the methodology robust. The importance of these methodologies is twofold. First, they offer a sound way to test theories expressed in the language of continuous-time nonlinear Markov processes. Second, they are easily integrated into the current framework of finance theory.

Most forecasting methodologies in use, including neural networks and other learning algorithms, offer point forecasts. These are difficult to integrate into the prevalent risk management technology which is frequently based on continuous-time representations. Methodologies for estimating directly parameters in Markov processes can, however, be easily integrated. Consider interest-rate models. The no-arbitrage framework imposes constraints to make term structure models compatible with the present term structure. The future evolution of interest rates (i.e., the actual forecast of interest rates) might, however, be unconstrained in multifactor models.

Conley, Hansen, Luttmer, and Scheinkman (1997) showed how to estimate the evolution of interest rates starting from actual interest rate data. They represent interest rates as subordinated diffusions, i.e., as diffusions subordinated to a stochastic change in the time scale. It is likely that these methodologies will have an impact on interest-rate representation. The need to shift attention to the forecasting ability of interest-rate models was cited by Thomas Daula, a managing director of global risk management at Bankers Trust.

7.6 MARKET MICROSTRUCTURE AND THEORY REDUCTION

This and the following subchapters explore questions of the interpretation of economic and finance theory and of theory reduction in economics. The general perspective is that economics, like physics, is made up of different levels of theory. Higher level theories can eventually be *reduced* to more basic theories through a process of logical deduction and statistical aggregation. Theories are distinguished not only by their mathematical form, but also by the set of observables that gives them empirical content. General equilibrium models are abstract models based on variational principles. Under specific assumptions, they can be inferred, through a process of theory reduction, from more basic models that describe agent behavior in operational terms.

Standard general equilibrium models are based on the notions of rational economic behavior and rational agents. Agent rationality means that agents maximize some object function. Each agent is thus characterized by a utility function defined over all economic variables, all instants of time, and all states of the economy. Utility is therefore a functional, i.e., a function defined on a space of functions. Agent decisions maximize the expected value of utility, assuming given stochastic processes for the economic variables (i.e., a probability structure on the state space).

In the strict neoclassical scheme, utility functions are assumed to describe some stable characteristic of the market. Utility functions are, therefore, assumed to be time-invariant: if a system is translated in time, utility functions remain the same; no feedback is allowed. This notion presents a number of conceptual difficulties but the essence, as remarked by Thomas Sargent, David Rockefeller professor of economics at the University of Chicago and a pioneer of rational expectations, is that the rational framework is static and stationary.

An economic system is in equilibrium if each agent can optimize his or her utility function independently and markets clear. For reasons related to the notion of rational expectations that will be discussed later, it is assumed that, in equilibrium, the objective stochastic process that describes economic variables is the same that appears under the maximization operator of each agent. Utility maximization is, therefore, the mathematical representation of the laws of motion of the system.

The utility maximization paradigm is quite abstract: it is the expression of laws of motion through variational principles. From a mathematical point of view, utility maximization can be looked at from different perspectives. If utility functions are given, it is possible to compute equilibrium price processes. If, however, price processes are given, one can compute the associated utility functions. While existence theorems can be established in both cases, there is no assurance of unicity of solutions; many examples of multiple equilibria are known and there are infinite ways of constructing rational equilibria.

In the physical sciences, many systems can be described through variational principles, i.e., the optimization of some functional. In classical mechanics, for instance, the equilibrium behavior of a system can be described by the so-called "principle of least energy" which is the minimization of the energy functional. Variational principles such as the principle of least energy are, of course, only convenient mathematical formulations; they do not imply that a physical system actually computes the functional to be minimized.

In the same way, the description of markets and agents through the maximization of expected utility might be interpreted as a way of formally characterizing the stochastic processes that describe the economy. Rationality is only a formal way of describing agents' decisions; unless some special rationality restriction is placed on utility functions, agents cannot be "irrational."

We can now turn our attention to how general equilibrium models can be empirically ascertained. As observed by Hansen and Scheinkman, the empirical content of these models needs to be reassessed. In fact, in standard general equilibrium models there is no operational definition of utility related to agents. In the language of modern science, an *operational* concept — in particular the operational definition of quantitative variables — is a concept that can be associated with a specific set of operations or measurements.

Utility functions can be observed only through mathematical inference from the market processes that utility maximization is supposed to explain. In other words, the only observables are the variables under the optimization operator, i.e., the aggregate market data such as price and volume. Agents are simply a convenient logical construction for formalizing processes; no independent observable characterizes agents.

If general equilibrium models were scientifically validated, this would not pose a problem. A specific set of utility functions descriptive of well determined sectors of the economy would be known and validated through a large number of empirical observations. Though abstract, these utility functions would be known to yield an equilibrium solution to all processes encountered in the economy.

This is far from being the case. There is no unified, validated set of utility functions to describe different sectors of the economy. The general equilibrium paradigm is regarded as a broad framework, to be adapted to different situations. This broad adaptability is the empirical indeterminacy referred to previously.

The next step is therefore to understand if and how general equilibrium theories can be enriched to allow utility functions to correspond to independent observables in an operational way. Hansen and Heckman, as we have seen, proposed to enrich economic theory in some fundamental sense, thereby rendering operationally meaningful the concept of agent utility in general equilibrium theories.

In general terms, the question can be formulated to ask what variables and observations are required to describe the economy. The economy might be described by a set of variables and models richer than standard general equilibrium but still at the aggregate level. The novelty is that a body of research is focused on finding operationally defined models of the agent decision-making process and the interaction between agents. These models require not only operational variables related to the measurement of utility or other aggregate functions, but also the explicit characterization of *actual* agent information processing.

As a consequence, we are seeing the emergence of economic explanations based on micro rules. Through logical and statistical processes, these rules might then be reduced to aggregate rules that may or may not be general equilibrium models formulated in terms of utility functions. The latter would give us a logical link between an abstract utility function and a description of real-world agents.

Underlining this point, Prof. Kirman remarks that research on the economy as a complex evolving system is based on today's models of the agent decision-making process. In a number of situations, he observes, these models might indeed approximate rational behavior. In fact, Prof. Kirman notes, after determining realistic decision-making processes, we can study how systems will actually evolve under those rules. This evaluation might also be described through the rational agent optimization paradigm.

Theory reduction is an important process in the physical sciences where the most widely studied example is thermodynamics. During the last century, thermodynamics developed as an independent science based on describing macroscopic systems through quantities such as heat, temperature, and entropy. Its development was due to the need to explain a number of phenomena that could not be explained within the framework of classical mechanics.

At the end of the last century, thanks to the pioneering work of the German physicist Georg Boltzman, it was demonstrated that all the laws of thermodynamics could be explained through statistical mechanics. It was, in fact, established that the laws of thermodynamics could be derived from those of classical mechanics, assuming that macroscopic systems were made up of a large number of microscopic particles that follow classical mechanical laws plus *statistical bridging principles*. Thermodynamics was thereby reduced to classical mechanics plus statistics.

The notion of theory reduction is invoked every time macroscopic theories are explained in terms of microscopic laws that govern microscopic particles. For instance, the laws of chemistry could, in principle and with some caveat, be reduced to quantum mechanics. Theory reduction has recently been invoked to explain biological and psychological laws in terms of physical laws. There might, nevertheless, be logical limits to the reduction process.

The notion of theory reduction is important to understanding the path from rational optimizing behavior to complex learning behavior. Rational optimizing behavior is a broad abstract framework that leaves agent decision rules operationally unspecified. If agent decision-making processes are effectively modeled through micro models that are associated to agent observables, we reach a different level of explanation.

Understanding whether or not rational optimizing behavior can be recovered starting from micro laws becomes a question of theory reduction. This might be possible under special hypotheses. In general, a utility optimization framework is stationary and does not allow for learning, but as remarked by Prof. Kirman, it has been shown that even a learning framework might end up originating a behavior of macro quantities that can be described by agent optimality.

Alternatively, the rational optimizing agent paradigm could be broadened to include more general optimal control variational principles. This would allow to explain the evolution of macro variables. Agent micro rules with learning can be reduced to this broader paradigm.

7.7 MODELS AND MODEL INTERPRETATION

An oft-raised question is what knowledge a rational agent is assumed to have. The rational optimizing paradigm is frequently criticized on the grounds that it attributes infinite knowledge to agents. This is a delicate point that needs discussion.

A real agent decides on the basis of finite decision-making processes. These processes are based on, among other, forecasts calculated on past data. If these processes were scientifically known for each agent in the market, then the economist could study, in abstract terms, the price processes that originate from these agents under different assumptions.

It might be found that under some conditions the resulting processes can still be abstractly described by a rational utility maximization paradigm. Prof. Kirman remarks that agents might be described by a utility maximization paradigm even if their real decision-making process is only boundedly rational, i.e., even if agents can make only limited forecasts.

This mathematical description does not imply that agents necessarily "know" the processes originated by their actions. To make a physical analogy, a molecule in a thin film of water that forms on top of a glass does not need to "know" the principle of energy minimization that describes its behavior and, therefore, the shape of the film.

The scientific knowledge acquired by studying the agent decision-making process and its effects on market prices feeds back into the decision-making process itself. But this feedback is not simple and straight-forward. Market macro laws might carry an intrinsic uncertainty, limiting their usefulness to agents. Agents might nevertheless interpret and specialize laws in various ways, with different levels of mathematical and computational skills.

Muth (1961) first observed explicitly that to develop a tenable theory of economic behavior it must be admitted that agents share the same knowledge as the econometrician describing them. There is, however, no need to make the hypothesis that scientific knowledge about price processes feeds back into agent decision making in a uniform and immediate way.

Consider the physical world. Despite our high level of knowledge of physical laws, products are highly diversified. This is due to the many design options that implement specific trade-offs and to the limited and unequal distribution of skills. Likewise in finance, though knowledge is acquired and shared among agents, decision-making processes can be highly heterogeneous.

The discussion related to the knowledge and information required by an optimizing agent remains on an abstract level. It has little empirical meaning and might not be fruitful. The real problem, from the empirical point of view, is whether the rational optimizing model is applicable or not for describing empirical data, how it can be made empirically meaningful, and whether it is compatible with detailed operational models of agent decision-making processes and market information structures.

If economic laws were known with the same level of precision as the laws of physics, this discussion would be quite meaningless. Economists would know if and when an optimizing paradigm applies and would be able to establish market micro laws. Agent decision-making processes could be reduced to some macro rules. The knowledge of the economist would be scientifically validated and optimization processes could be carried out.

We are, nevertheless, still quite far from a detailed theory that can be tested empirically with precision close to that of physics. In this situation, as remarked by the University of Chicago's Prof. Scheinkman, we might have to be content with more modest goals, such as being able to understand broad structural characteristics of the economy. It is likely that there are lower bounds to the uncertainty entailed by the scientific knowledge of price processes.

7.8 SELF-REFERENTIALITY AND RATIONAL EXPECTATIONS

We have explored questions related to the interpretation of economic laws, showing that equilibrium models based on the maximization of expected utility can be interpreted as abstract models of the market. Through a process of theory reduction and under specific hypotheses, the same models can also be logically derived from models of the decision-making process of single agents. We will now explore how equilibrium models are related to the question of the self-referentiality of the economy. The perspective here is that self-referentiality is a general concept; the rational expectations hypothesis is one way, albeit extreme, of solving the problems it poses.

Any theory that links the time evolution of economic quantities to agent behavior must take into account the self-referentiality of the economy. The economy is self-referential because economic agents act in function of their forecasts of the future development of the economy, thereby influencing the evolution that they themselves had forecast.

A distinction should be made between self-referentiality and the question of the modelability of human behavior. The latter is not the issue of self-referentiality. It is sometimes argued that the economy cannot be modeled as it deals, ultimately, with human behavior and human behavior cannot be modeled. From a mathematical point of view, this statement means that the human decision-making process is a random process. In the parlance of algorithmic information theory, we should say that human decisions are not "algorithmically compressible."

The question of the mathematical modelability of human behavior is a difficult issue with a long history of philosophical debate. It is clouded by questions concerning free will, morals, and rationality. On a true scientific level, it is difficult to understand just what are the *elementary particles* of the human behavior to model. Are they words? Elementary actions? Or is human behavior a continuum without atoms?

From the point of view of economics, human behavior is reasonably well delimited. It might therefore be possible to say that we know what the elementary economic decisions are. Few would maintain that human economic behavior is completely random. Still, many would argue that it is impossible to predict the outcome of individual critical decisions.

It is fair to say that there is agreement that economic behavior is modelable in a probabilistic sense, with large areas of uncertainty. In economic models based on the theory of multiagent systems, agents are modeled through mathematical tools including artificial intelligence algorithms and statistical decision rules. Uncertainty is generally captured through the distribution of different decision rules.

Let's now go back to the question of self-referentiality. In abstract terms, a self-referential system is a system whose evolution modifies the laws of motion that describe the system's evolution. The economy is self-referential as it follows laws of motion that agents learn. In learning, agents modify the economy, modifying thereby the laws of motion themselves. Providing feedback from the market, learning forces the economy into self-referentiality.

Self-referentiality is not specific to economics, but is found in many domains, including physics and mathematical logic. Self-referential behavior is found in chemistry where the laws of a chemical reaction depend on the mix of the components that react. As the reaction progresses, the mix of components changes and the laws of the reaction change in consequence. Though this example might seem easy to solve and far from the complex reality of economics, it is instructive as it shows the key elements of self-referentiality: the mutual interaction between a system and its environment.

There are different strategies for solving the problem of self-referentiality in the description of phenomena. The simplest — well known from the physical sciences — is to constrain models to situations of equilibrium. Equilibrium resolves self-referentiality by imposing coherence between the laws of motion and the relative environment.

In the case of a chemical reactor, a situation of equilibrium arises when the supply of reactants and the removal of heat and of the products of the reaction are what is needed to keep the reaction going, thus holding stable the mix in the environment. In the economy, a situation of equilibrium arises when forecasted prices are the same as those produced by the mutual interaction of agents.

A more general strategy is to adopt dynamic laws that take into account the changes produced by motion. Often this implies going from steady-state laws to dynamic laws that describe the instantaneous rate of change of phenomena. Solving self-referentiality is a question of the model level: one might confine attention to equilibrium models, or adopt models of a higher level able to encompass the entire dynamic of the system.

In the case of a chemical reactor in equilibrium, one needs to know only the laws of chemical reactions under constant pressure, temperature, and components mix. In a dynamic environment, however, an understanding of how all these parameters are interconnected is required. Similarly, in a situation of market equilibrium, one needs to know only simplified laws of the relationship between stable prices and stable learning parameters; in a dynamic situation, an understanding of how learning rules change in function of price evolution is required.

Self-referentiality and equilibrium appear at, and are solved at, different levels of model complexity and grainings of time. A complex dynamic law of motion might be adopted to solve a problem of mutual interaction with the environment. But this new law might, in its turn, be subject to the problem of self-referentiality in an augmented context. Over longer periods, however, statistical equilibrium might be restored.

In a neoclassical economic model, the laws of motion that characterize each agent are represented by expected utility maximization. In equilibrium, the processes over which expected utility is maximized must coincide with those that result from utility maximization. This is the notion of rational expectations in economics.

That forecasted processes (i.e., the processes that appear under the maximization operators) and the actual processes are identical is the essential characterization of a rational expectations equilibrium. Rational expectations is, University of Chicago professor Thomas Sargent says, agent optimality plus self-referentiality.

As the optimizing environment is assumed to be time invariant, a consequence of rational expectations equilibrium is the absence of feedback. But a rational expectations equilibrium is not logically incompatible with learning; it was noted above that agent optimality might be compatible with micro laws of boundedly rational agent decision-making processes. Prof. Sargent observes that some learning schemes under conditions of stationarity might result in a rational expectations equilibrium.

It would nevertheless be possible to define equilibrium without the identity of forecasted and actual processes, assuming that agents do not learn, i.e., assuming that they might be consistently wrong. This is often taken, wrongly, as a defense of rational expectations. In the absence of rational expectations, the argument goes, we have to admit that agents might be permanently biased in their expectations.

This is not so. Backing off rational expectations does not mean that agents are permanently biased, but that a different descriptive framework must be adopted. In particular, it has to be admitted that agents do not work in a situation of equilibrium. Agents are sometimes right, sometimes wrong. Over long periods of time, the economic system might be in a sort of statistical equilibrium, but it should be noted that this eventual statistical equilibrium is *not* the same as the classical rational equilibrium.

Figure 7.2 illustrates the relationship between agent optimality, equilibrium, and agent bounded rationality: a rational expectations equilibrium is agent optimality with self-referentiality. There is, in addition, an area of overlapping between micro decision rules (i.e., boundedly rational agent behavior rules) and rational expectations.

Agent optimality and rational expectations equilibrium on one side, and operational boundedly rational agent decision-making rules on the other are two *different descriptive frameworks*. The question of the *reduction* of the one to the other is not a question of principles, but one that needs to be investigated for each specific class of models.

Figure 7.2
A rational expectations equilibrium is agent optimality with self-referentiality.

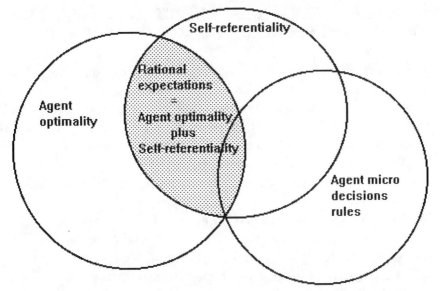

Prof. Sargent remarks that rational expectations is a broad framework that "gave theory power," allowing the explanation of a number of economic phenomena in a stable environment. It has worked well, he says, in studying the financial markets of developed countries where he puts the stable behavior at around 90%, but is not applicable when confronted with regime change, e.g., post-Communist Russia. Prof. Sargent notes, however, that even in mature markets a number of phenomena are difficult to explain within a rational expectations framework. Among these he mentions the seemingly large equity risk premia, the steepness of interest rates, and the real business cycle model.

Prof. Sargent observes that most research to solve puzzles like those cited has been done within the framework of rational expectations. Though is not impossible to explain these phenomena in a rational expectations framework (as noted above a theory can always be adjusted to explain a finite set of data), a dynamic framework might be more effective. A scientific solution is required. Prof. Sargent cites the need to get something "practical, reasonable" to use when the rational expectations hypothesis doesn't work and refers to new paradigms under construction.

7.9 BACKING OFF RATIONAL EXPECTATIONS: LEARNING, MULTIAGENT SYSTEMS, AND NONLINEAR DYNAMICS

Changes in macroeconomic thinking follow several lines, but all call for relaxing the rational expectations hypothesis and for adopting a complex-systems approach. For Prof. Sargent, a pioneer in the development of rational expectations, there are a lot of ways to back off rational expectations. "The problem," he notes, "is to do so in a disciplined way, introducing small perturbations." He suggests doing statistics in a conservative way, and advises asking the question: What if we don't have enough information on a probability distribution? This, Prof. Sargent says, leads to caution and worst-case analysis.

Commenting on research to relax rational expectations, University of Chicago professor Lars Hansen says that introducing small perturbations away from rational expectations allows economic actors to use models that are a simplification of the environment plus robustness concerns. Noting its success in other sectors, Prof. Hansen believes that robust control theory might bring to economics and finance a richer set of tools with some of the attractive features of the rational expectations paradigm plus the ability to accommodate complex decision making.

Brock and Hommes (1997) observe that there are two competing ways to explain the fluctuations in economies and financial markets. The neoclassical approach holds that, markets being rational and transparent, fluctuations are due (solely) to exogenous sources. The Keynesian approach maintains that there are endogenous sources of fluctuations. According to William Brock, William F. Vilas research professor of economics at the University of Wisconsin-Madison, chains of correlations create endogenous jumps. Modeling these jumps with the tools of statistical mechanics and multiple interacting agents will, he believes, result in a more faithful modeling of reality.

Let's now look more closely at different lines of research. Prof. Kirman at the University of Aix-Marseille, remarks that the rational expectations hypothesis is really just a convenient (and too simplistic) way of describing equilibrium. He reformulates the key question, asking: How do people learn? By studying learning and adaptation, the hope is that we can arrive at a better understanding of how agents and markets adapt to new situations, leading to a better model of economic processes. Research into learning follows two lines: (1) the study of human behavior and (2) the study of learning as information processing.

Studies on cognitive psychology focus on behavior, exploring how people process empirical evidence and form expectations. These studies show how biases such as over-confidence or loss aversion lead to less than rational judgement. The effects of regret have also been studied, showing how people judge decisions under uncertainty on the outcome and tend to change a good decision-making process because of bad outcomes.

Richard Thaler, Robert P. Gwinn professor of behavioral science and economics at the University of Chicago Graduate School of Business, applied cognitive psychology to the investment process, explaining a number of findings that would be difficult to explain under the assumption of the unbiased rationality of investors. Among these, Prof. Thaler and co-researchers offered a behavioral explanation for the success of contrarian strategies (see De Bondt and Thaler, 1995).

Behavioral theories enrich the empirical content of economics in essential ways. Most findings of behavioral psychology are not specific to economics or finance theory but refer to a broad spectrum of human behavior and its biases. The empirical content is obvious. The applicability of behavioral psychology to finance is an empirical question. Behavioral psychology deals with micro rules and cannot be directly compared with the optimizing agent paradigm.

The other line of research, which studies learning as information processing, focuses on the modeling of agent behavior as mathematical learning defined through artificial intelligence concepts. Agents are modeled as intelligent information processing systems. Sargent (1993) offers a broad view of artificial intelligence methods in the context of bounded rationality.

Blake LeBaron's work on applying an intelligent agent approach to technical trading rules was mentioned above. Commenting on the difficulties in modeling intelligent agents at the macroeconomic level, Prof. LeBaron notes that the problem is in getting the many relationships and information flows correct. "If some relationships or information flows are missed," he says, "models might be wrong." Prof. LeBaron notes that modeling individual markets is easier: it's clear where the relationships are and intervalidating between different markets is less important. "The need," he adds, "is to understand the appropriate small-scale unit to explore and getting the interconnection lines correct."

Another research effort focuses on modeling the economy as a complex multiagent system. Prof. Kirman (1997) observes that there are different paradigms for agent interaction. One is a Walrasian paradigm where the only signal is the market price and agents optimize in isolation in function of the price process. This model is abstract and does not explain how prices are formed.

Another paradigm is a game theoretic approach where each agent interacts directly with every other agent. This approach could, at least in principle, be made operational as it implies only the knowledge of how each other agent effectively processes information. It is not, however, a realistic paradigm: agents do not know exactly how other agents react; the reasoning involved is extremely complicated.

Prof. Kirman advocates an intermediate paradigm in which agents have only bounded rationality and interact with each other in a structured way. This, he says, is what happens in the real world where agents act on the basis of limited knowledge of other agents as broad aggregates. Prof. Kirman studied price formation under spontaneous agent aggregation in the Marseille fish market and the Moscow street market. With bounded rationality models and agent aggregation, we come closer to a true description of agent behavior and our ability to perform observations is enriched.

University of Chicago professor of economics José Scheinkman is conducting research on multiagent systems and social interaction. Working in the area of crime, he asks why crime rates vary so much even if economic and social variables are similar. The objective is to understand how things are mediated, not through aggregation, but how individual interactions can change the outcome. At the heart of the matter, Prof. Scheinkman says, are information and belief flows. While the focus of Prof. Scheinkman's research is not the financial markets, arriving at a better understanding of information and belief flows might lead to a better understanding of the behavior of market participants.

Many of the methods used in modeling multiagent systems are borrowed from nonequilibrium statistical mechanics. (For an introduction to statistical mechanics, see Appendix A.7.2; for a thorough handling of the subject, see Aoki, 1996.) Statistical mechanics provides a framework for the description of multiequilibria as many microscopic states are compatible with the same macroscopic states. It also provides the analytical framework for projecting individual relationships between agents onto macroeconomic behavior. It does so through the formalism of *master equations*. The projection process can be carried out at different levels of coarse graining of information, a feature that proved highly useful in the physical sciences.

Based on previous research, Prof. Brock (1993) developed a general theory of how to describe the probabilistic setting of interacting particle systems and discusses the application of mean field theory, a mathematical technology to coarse grain the effects of interaction between agents. He shows how rich dynamic behavior can emerge in these multiagent systems.

In later work with his colleague at the University of Wisconsin-Madison Steven Durlauf, Prof. Brock (1997) focused on the problem of discrete choices with interaction. Extending previous work on the theory of social interactions, they show how aggregation phenomena emerge in complex multiagent structures. The theoretical work was then applied to empirical studies.

Brock and Hommes (1996) introduced the concept (and model) of Adaptive Rational Equilibrium Dynamics (ARED). In the ARED model, agents are free to choose from a finite set of different predictors or expectation functions. The model thereby allows the generation of rich dynamics, including different types of chaotic behavior, while still allowing the imposition of equilibrium conditions.

Commenting on the ARED model, Prof. Brock says that it provides the insight that there are phases when the economy strays away from rational expectations and phases when equilibrium forces pull it back. When close to equilibrium, Prof. Brock observes, buying rational expectations is not worth it, but everyone's doing this produces shifts away from equilibrium. These build up, oscillation occurs, and it becomes worthwhile to have predicted when the oscillation would have occurred. People, Prof. Brock remarks, then start to switch back to buying rational expectations and equilibrium is re-established. "There is," he adds, "a need to nest rational expectations in a different framework of heterogeneous agents and of different time horizons."

Some researchers have used the opinion aggregation approach to explain the price formation process through phenomena of the stochastic clustering of opinion. Among them, Thomas Lux (1996) at the University of Bamberg proposed an explanation for ARCH behavior based on opinion aggregation.

Yet another approach attempts to develop deterministic descriptions of the economy as a nonlinear *chaotic* system. The reasoning behind this approach lies in the findings of chaos theory, i.e., the theory of nonlinear dynamical systems. Among the findings is the observation that very complex behavior might arise from simple differential equations or even finite maps. By "very complex" is meant that trajectories might come arbitrarily close at an instant and diverge thereafter. In other words, very small differences in initial conditions might produce very large divergence at some later point in time. This observation, first made by the MIT meteorologist Edward Lorentz in 1963, has since produced a rich theory of dynamical systems.

An interesting finding about the behavior of chaotic systems is that their trajectories cluster around *attractors* in the state space of the systems. Under well established mathematical conditions, it is possible to reconstruct the attractor from a finite number of observations.

These and other findings suggested describing the economy as a nonlinear dynamical system. The implication is that the economy evolves as a deterministic system; the perceived randomness in economic behavior would be the manifestation of chaotic behavior. Through a careful selection of variables made possible by the tools of chaos theory, it was hoped that it would be possible to arrive at an approximate deterministic description of the economy.

Caution is, however, necessary. Prof. LeBaron remarks that the type of nonlinearities found in economics are different from those found in physics. He likens nonlinearities in economics to the opening of a safe: the right combination is required to produce the desired outcome, i.e., the opening of the safe; any other combination has no effect.

Research has attempted to find evidence of chaotic behavior in the economy. This is tricky because, as Prof. Brock observes, nonlinearities do not necessarily imply chaos. Brock (1993) — who is also an external professor at the Santa Fe Institute — explored ways to detect and model a vast class of nonlinear and chaotic behavior. He shows how tests for linearity and independence can be applied in a variety of empirical contexts and outlines mathematical strategies for handling systems formed by many particles with links.

Though the evidence of deterministic chaos in economic times series is presently scant, it is possible — even easy — to build mathematical models of markets that exhibit chaotic behavior. Purely classical models, as the above-mentioned multiagent model developed by Prof. Brock and co-researchers, can exhibit chaos.

It is fair to say that, although applying chaos theory to economic and finance theory has proved more difficult than anticipated, chaos theory has made a lasting contribution. Commenting on what nonlinear dynamics has brought to finance, Prof. Scheinkman notes that it is now accepted that to understand the evolution of, e.g., interest rates, one must be able to explain phenomena such as nonlinear drifts and volatilities. He adds that while chaos theory is not a method for prediction or tools to make money on the markets, it does help in understanding how factors are related to each other over time. Prof. Scheinkman began work in applying nonlinear dynamics to economics in the early 1980s and is an external professor at the Santa Fe Institute, which pioneered research in complex systems.

Developments in learning, nonlinear dynamics, and multiagent systems will have an impact on risk management. New concepts are in fact needed to explain critical economic phenomena. Not only are developed economies venturing into new and unexplored markets, but the production and consumption structure of economies is changing.

None of this is really new: venturing into new markets has been a constant in human activity, and production and consumption schemes undergo continual change. The Late Middle Ages-Renaissance and the Industrial Revolution are two periods that witnessed a radical change in production and consumption patterns. But the *quantitative* side of present changes is unparalleled. Information processing, for instance, has multiplied millionfold the information output of society in the last fifty years. The question of just what is output and how to measure it might need to be reassessed. These phenomena are highly nonlinear and subject to self-sustaining criticalities.

7.10 NEW DIRECTIONS IN MACROECONOMIC MODELING

The push towards a macroeconomic approach to risk management is related to a shift in risk management from a control function to a financial optimization function and the consequent lengthening of the time horizon. Commenting on the role of macroeconomics in finance, University of Wisconsin professor of economics Blake LeBaron notes that if the objective is to have a point forecast a week or two out, macroeconomics just adds noise. "But," he says, "if the objective is to forecast one year out, taking into consideration tail probabilities, then macro data might add a lot."

The major source of macroeconomic quantitative methods — econometrics — implements macroeconomic modeling based on statistical theory. Macroeconomic theory is still quite far from being able to provide a reasonably accurate explanation for and prediction of economic events. Its modeling is based on linear approximations and suffers from the same limits as finance theory: a broad theory, it needs to be restricted and specified to be made empirically verifiable. When specified, however, it does not match empirical data.

An additional problem is the aggregates considered in macroeconomic theory. These need to be reassessed. How, for instance, can the physical output of an economy be measured? Macroeconomics assumes that physical output changes only slowly in time, so that it is meaningful to study economic dynamics with models whose structure does not change too much. But this is not the case in many situations.

University of Aix-Marseille professor of economics Alan Kirman observes that macroeconomics typically tries to do everything with a few variables, e.g., inflation, GNP. But Prof. Kirman questions if it is possible to forecast with just a few variables. There is, he believes, the need to go beyond simple relationships, looking at more structure and at more and higher dimensions (e.g., What is the structure of income distribution? of unemployment? of trade? What are the time horizons of traders?). "If you don't know how the system works," Prof. Kirman adds, "you can't model." He notes the importance of observing what happens in markets, the links, i.e., who talks to whom, who buys from whom, and how the links change over time. These relationships can, Prof. Kirman says, set off phenomena such as chain reactions, self-generation, and herd-like movements.

An important issue for risk management is the handling of the notion of value in finance theory and in macroeconomics. In finance, value is market value; in macroeconomics, value is the real output of the economy as determined by the measurement of production aggregates.

The *reality* of these aggregates is elucidated by the notion of inflation which tends to distinguish between the increase of solid physical output and the speculative push of markets. In classical thinking, the link between the two is provided by the information processing ability of the markets. Markets filter and weigh information, assigning values that correspond to the real economy; they are held to implement rational expectations.

The soundness of these notions vis-à-vis markets that increment their total value at rates well above the growth of the real economy is, perhaps, questionable. What is needed, from the point of view of risk management, is some theory able to reconcile a market approach with a real-economy approach in systems that change rapidly in their qualitative and quantitative aspects. Advances in macroeconomic modeling might be able to provide a unified handling of economies driven by market mechanisms. Though most work is being done in academia, the requirement to better manage risk should give further impetus to research.

A theory of risk, in its most developed form, is nothing less than a full-fledged theory of economic phenomena, but it stops short of a complete theory of the future development of the economy: there is just too much uncertainty. Nevertheless, a theory that allows to describe and predict how the economy responds to inputs would be a significant step forward. It implies viewing the economy at a level where is becomes a stable physical system, capturing the structure responsible for the stable behavior. Learning and statistical physics are presently the most likely candidates for such an endeavor. Combined with fresh insight in macroeconomics, they might provide the framework that would allow for the more faithful modeling of both the real economy and the markets.

7.11 MANAGING OPERATIONS RISK

Risk management methodologies have focused on market and credit risk. But other types of risk can be significant. Among these are operations risk, political or social risk and the risk of collapse of an economic system.

Operations risk has been widely publicized following large losses at major financial firms. There are questions as regards the ability to model operations risk and to integrate it into a global risk management system. It would be a mistake, however, to think of modeling operations risk as a stochastic process. As Carol Alexander, researcher in time-series analysis at the University of Sussex, put it, "operations risk cannot be boiled down to a variance-covariance matrix." It is, she says, primarily a qualitative issue. Dr. Alexander suggests doing critical path analysis, using the tools of operations research, e.g., flow charts, decision trees.

Financial firms expose themselves to market risk because of the premium associated with it; banks expose themselves to credit risk, intrinsic to their activity, because of the associated gains. Operations risk, on the other hand, is a pure loss. The objective is to eliminate it. The modeling of operations risk is the modeling of a decision-making structure with its information flows and operations. The challenge is in how to reduce to a minimum the possibility of "surprises" within the structure.

GAT president Thomas Ho addresses the problem of operations risk within the framework of what he calls the investment-quality cycle concept. This concept, proposed by GAT as a suite of consulting and software modules, likens the investment management process to a manufacturing process, and the modeling is similar.

The study of complex systems might shed light on questions of organizations insofar as it explains the formation of aggregation and structure in groups. For instance, one problem in designing hedging strategies is that there is a tendency for people inside a firm to share views. The result: everyone gets caught with the same book. At a higher level of aggregation, similar phenomena may be at work in the markets themselves. From the point of view of risk management, there is the need to hedge exposures to views. Research on multiagent systems may be useful here. Reference was made earlier to research on multiagent models and social interaction.

An interesting use of nonlinear methods applied to the markets is pattern detection. The use of neural networks to find patterns to exploit for profit in specific financial markets has received a lot of attention. Prof. Scheinkman notes that perhaps an even more interesting use of nonlinear methods for finding patterns is in areas where their use does not destroy the pattern, at least not in the short-run.

One such area is in detecting patterns in trading for performance evaluation or fraud detection. The London Stock Exchange, for instance, installed a system to detect insider trading on the

Exchange. Developed by the London-based software firm Search-Space, the system uses a combination of adaptive (learning) methods including neural networks, fuzzy logic, and genetic algorithms.

7.12 POLITICAL AND SOCIAL RISK

Risk due to political or social change or to the failure of an economic system, must be distinguished from market catastrophes such as the large and sudden market movements in developed economies. There is some experience, albeit limited from a quantitative point of view, of crashes in established markets. There is a notion of diversification strategies and post-crash behavior. Macroeconomics might help in understanding long-term equilibrium conditions.

New emerging markets or systems undergoing structural change pose challenges of a different nature. They can collapse for reasons difficult to foresee and to model quantitatively. Standard financial modeling, even with appropriately large risk parameters, cannot be adopted: there are insufficient statistical data and internal criticalities might be overwhelming. Commenting on the applicability of rational expectations to nonstationary situations, Prof. Sargent remarks that when confronted with regime change, rational expectations is not applicable.

As the risk premia in these markets are high, the level of interest in modeling risk due to unrecoverable failures is also high. There is, presently, little theory to support the modeling; the decision-making process is highly judgemental. Still this is an area that could greatly benefit from complex-systems modeling. In fact, in emerging markets agents cannot learn fast enough to cope with the changing environment.

7.13 CLOSING REMARKS

This book has explored the theoretical framework of and the methodologies used in risk management. The discipline is clearly in a phase of intense research and rapid development. The "agent of change" is the shift from risk management as a control function to risk management as an optimization function. This shift will have consequences on the organizational structure and modus operandi of banks and financial institutions.

There will be changes at the level of organization due to the growing importance of scientific skills. Some of these changes are difficult to forecast. Yong Li, risk manager at Credit Lyonnais Americas, remarks that risk management is presently in the critical phase of establishing itself as a part of an organization. Five or ten years down the road, he says, risk management may diversify into different business units or become a truly indispensable unit. Either way, Mr. Li says, its value to the firm will increase.

Balance sheet management will be transformed; decisions will be increasingly guided — eventually made — by a global validated statistical decision-making process. But a word of caution is necessary: simplicity constraints must be applied. The introduction of scientific methodologies in banking and finance is recent. The requisite cultural shift presents challenges that should not be underestimated.

There is a paradox in economics. Considered a scientific challenge given the complexity of the system — economics was listed among the twelve *Grand Challenges* of the National Science Foundation's scientific program — in practice, economics and finance are still managed primarily with human judgement and a little mathematics.

But it would be a mistake to relegate scientific research in economics to the domain of academic research, void of practical consequences. The progress of science and technology is highly nonlinear. Awakenings can be rude. We have seen this in sector after sector.

This last chapter has tried to anticipate developments in economics that make use of highly sophisticated science. The key change is not in the mathematical methods themselves, but in the relationship between mathematical modeling and empirical data. Until very recently, macroeconomic modeling such as growth theory was considered little more than a "parable," to use Nobel prize-winner Robert Solow's term.

What is new — and of practical importance — is the development of economics as a true empirical science. As we have seen, some of the largest financial firms are putting the accent on data. The availability of data and the modeling of empirical data will change the world of economics and finance. The promise is that improving our ability to model the real economy will improve our ability to manage risk.

References

Aoki, Masanao, *New Approaches to Macroeconomic Modeling*, Cambridge University Press, New York, NY, 1996.

Brock, William A., Josef Lakonishok and Blake LeBaron, "Simple Technical Trading Rules and the Stochastic Properties of Stock Returns," *Journal of Finance*, vol. XLVII, no. 5, December 1992.

Brock, William A., "Pathways to Randomness in the Economy; Emergent Nonlinearity and Chaos in Economics and Finance," *Estudios Economicos*, vol. 8, no. 1, Mexico, 1993.

Brock, William A. and Blake D. LeBaron, "A Dynamic Structural Model for Stock Return Volatility and Trading Volume," *Review of Economics and Statistics*, vol. 78, no. 1, p 94-110, February 1996.

Brock, William A., "Asset Price Behavior in Complex Environments," Working paper no. 9621, Social Systems Research Institute, University of Wisconsin-Madison, April 1996.

Brock, William A. and Cars H. Hommes, "A Rational Route to Randomness," Working paper no. 9530R, Social Systems Research Institute, University of Wisconsin-Madison, revised July 1996.

Brock, William A. and Cars H. Hommes, "Heterogeneous Beliefs and Routes to Chaos in a Simple Asset Pricing Model," Working paper no. 9621, Social Systems Research Institute, University of Wisconsin-Madison, August 1996.

Brock, William A., W.D. Dechert, Blake LeBaron and J.A. Scheinkman, "A Test for Independence Based on the Correlation Dimension," *Econometric Reviews*, vol. 15, no. 3, pp 197-235, 1996.

Brock, William and Steven N. Durlauf, "Discrete Choice with Social Interactions: II," Department of Economics, University of Wisconsin-Madison, 5 January 1997.

Brock, William A. and Cars H. Hommes, "Models of Complexity in Economics and Finance," Working paper no. 9706, Social Systems Research Institute, University of Wisconsin-Madison, April 1997.

Brock, William A. and Steven N. Durlauf, "A Formal Model of Theory Choice in Science," Working paper no. 9707, Social Systems Research Institute, University of Wisconsin-Madison, April 1997.

Conley, Timothy G., Lars Peter Hansen, Erzo G.J. Luttmer and José A. Scheinkman, "Short-Term Interest Rates as Subordinated Diffusions," University of Chicago, May 29, 1997.

De Bondt, Werner F.M. and Richard H. Thaler, "Financial Decision-Making in Markets and Firms: A Behavioral Perspective," Chapter 13 in *Handbooks in OR & MS*, R. Jarrow et al., Eds, Elsevier Science, 1995.

Feyerabend, Paul, *Against Method*, New Left Books, London, 1975.

Focardi, Sergio, "Adaptive Computational Methods in Economics: Questions of Scientific Methods in the Empirical Study of the Economy," *World Network World*, ed., M. Novàk, IDG-VSP, Prague, 1995.

Hansen, Lars Peter and José A. Scheinkman, "Back to the Future: Generating Moment Implications for Continuous-Time Markov Processes," *Econometrica*, vol. 63, no. 4, 767-804, July 1995.

Hansen, Lars Peter and James J. Heckman, "The Empirical Foundations of Calibration," *Journal of Economic Perspectives*, vol. 10, no. 1, 87-104, Winter 1996.

Hansen, Lars Peter, José A. Scheinkman and Nizar Touzi, "Spectral Methods for Identifying Scalar Diffusions," University of Chicago, 7 March 1997; forthcoming *Journal of Econometrics*.

Hansen, Lars Peter, Thomas J. Sargent and Thomas D. Tallarini Jr., "Robust Permanent Income and Pricing," University of Chicago, May 11 1997.

Harrison, J.M. and D. Kreps, "Martingales and Arbitrage in Multiperiod Securities Markets," *Journal of Economic Theory*, 20:381-408, 1979.

Kirman, Alan P., "Ants, Rationality and Recruitment," *Quarterly Journal of Economics*, 108:137-156, February, 1993.

Kirman, Alan P., "Economies with Interacting Agents," Working Paper G & WII, University of Bonn, 1995.

Kirman, Alan P., "The Market as an Interactive System," Working Paper, GREQAM, EHESS and the University of Aix-Marseille III, Marseille, 1997.

Kuhn, Thomas, *The Structure of Scientific Revolutions, 2nd edition*, University of Chicago Press, Chicago, IL, 1970.

LeBaron, Blake, "Chaos and Nonlinear Forecastability in Economics and Finance," *Philosophical Transactions of the Royal Society of London*, 348, pp 397-404, 1994.

Lux, Thomas, "Time-variation of Second Moments from a Multi-agent Noise Trader Model of Financial Markets," Second International Conference on Computing in Economics and Finance, Geneva, 1996.

Madrigal, Vincent and José Scheinkman, "Price Crashes, Information Aggregation, and Market-Making," forthcoming *Journal of Economic Theory*.

Millonas, Mark, Editor, *Fluctuations and Order: The New Synthesis*, Springer-Verlag, New York, NY, 1996.

Mori, H, *Prog. Theoretical Physics*, 33:424+, 1965.

Muth, J.F., "Rational Expectations and the Theory of Price Movements," *Econometrica*, 29:315-335, 1961.

Sargent, Thomas J., *Macroeconomics*, Academic Press, San Diego, CA, 1987.

Sargent, Thomas J., *Bounded Rationality in Macroeconomics*, Claredon Press, Oxford, 1993.

Appendices

A.2.1 THE STOCHASTIC REPRESENTATION OF THE ECONOMY

In the stochastic description of financial markets, the economy is formally represented by a probability space $(\Omega, \mathbf{F}, P)$ where Ω is the set of possible states, $\mathbf{F}$ is the σ-algebra of events, and P is a probability measure. A σ-algebra is a non-empty class of subsets of Ω which is closed under the operation of complementation and denumerable union. A probability measure P is a real-valued set function defined over the sets of $\mathbf{F}$ that takes values in the interval $[0,1]$ such that $P(\Omega) = 1$ and $P(\cup A_i) = \sum A_i$ for any denumerable disjoint sequence of subsets A_i such that $\cup A_i \in \mathbf{F}$.

A key concept in the stochastic representation of the economy is information and its revelation through time. The progressive revelation of information is modeled by *partitions* and *filtrations*. Partitions are useful in the discrete case, less so in the continuous case. Given a set A, a family $\{A_i\}$, $i = 1, n$ of mutually disjoint subsets of A, such that $\cup A_i = A$, is called a partition of A. A partition $\{A_i\}$ is finer than a partition $\{B_j\}$ if every set B_j is the union of some A_i sets. In the discrete case, there are a finite number of instants and states and therefore of partitions.

The revelation of information is modeled as follows. Suppose that a partition of the set of states is associated to each instant and that, if $t < s$, the partition associated to the instant s is finer than that associated to the instant t. Partitions represent information. In fact, at each instant, it is known to which set of the corresponding partition the current state belongs. With the passing of time, information is revealed insofar as states are constrained to belong to ever smaller sets; at the end of the period, the state is fully revealed. The set of progressively finer partitions, each associated to an instant, is called an *information structure*.

The notion of partitions is intuitive but insufficient for handling probability. In addition, in the continuous case, partitions should contain an infinite number of sets, each with probability zero. Filtration is, therefore, a more convenient mathematical tool for modeling information and its revelation through time. A filtration is a family of sub σ-algebras $\{F_t\}$ that associates to each instant t a σ-algebra $F_t \subseteq F$. It is assumed that $\{F_t\}$ is a growing family of events in the sense that $t \leq s$ implies $F_t \subseteq F_s$. A probability space (Ω, F, P) equipped with a filtration $\{F_t\}$ is called a *filtered probability space*. A filtered probability space is written as the quadruple $(\Omega, F, \{F_t\}, P)$. Filtrations represent information as at each instant t it is known what sets in the corresponding F_t are true.

Prices, dividends, rates, and other economic quantities are defined as stochastic processes adapted to the filtration $\{F_t\}$. A stochastic process X adapted to the filtration $\{F_t\}$ is a time-dependent random variable X_t such that X_t is F_t-measurable for any instant t. This means that an adapted stochastic process X is a real-valued function of time t and states ω, i.e. X: $X(t,\omega) \Rightarrow R$ where R is the set of real numbers such that, for each value of t, the inverse image $X^{-1}(H)$ of any linear *Borel set* H belongs to F_t or, equivalently, that the sets $\{\omega: X(t,\omega) < x\}$ belong to F_t for any real number x.

For each ω, the function $X = X(t, \cdot)$ is called a path of the process X. States $\omega \in \Omega$ can then be identified with the set of paths of all stochastic processes that are assumed to characterize the economy. The assumption that stochastic processes are adapted to a filtration is a consistency condition that ensures that information is not revealed in anticipation.

In the discrete case, i.e., if the probability space consists of a finite number of states and if probabilities assume only a finite number of values, partitions and filtrations can be put in a one-to-one correspondence. Figure A.2.1.1 illustrates the notion of the propagation of information and the correspondence of partitions and filtrations in the discrete case; information is revealed through progressively finer partitions (left) and the corresponding filtrations (right).

A fundamental notion is that of conditional expectation, a generalization of the concept of conditional probability. Suppose that a σ-algebra F is given together with a sub σ-algebra G and that the random variable X is F-measurable. The conditional expectation of X given G, written as $E(X/G)$, is a G-measurable random variable such that $\int_G E(X/G)\, dP = \int_G X dP$ for each set $G \in G$. Given a filtration $\{F_t\}$, the conditional expectations $E_t(X) \equiv E(X/F_t)$ model the evolution of expectations with the revelation of information.

Figure A.2.1.1

Partitions and filtrations represent the revelation of information through time. At each instant t, it is revealed what events in F_t are true.

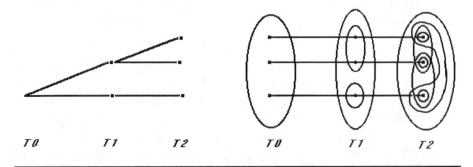

$T\theta$ $T1$ $T2$ $T\theta$ $T1$ $T2$

The conditional expectation of a random variable X given a random variable Z, $E(X/Z)$ is defined as the conditional expectation of X given the σ-algebra σ(Z) generated by Z: $E(X/Z) = E(X/\sigma(Z))$. The σ-algebra σ(Z) generated by a random variable Z is defined as the smallest σ-algebra with respect to which Z is measurable, i.e., the intersection of all the σ-algebras with respect to which Z is measurable.

The conditional expectation of X given Z can be interpreted as the average value of X known the value of Z. This concept cannot, however, be expressed through the usual concept of conditional probability as the conditioning event — the set of ωs that correspond to a given value of Z — will in general have probability zero. The definition of conditional expectation given above has therefore to be used. As $E(X/Z)$ is measurable with respect to the σ-algebra generated by Z, it is a function of Z: $E(X/Z) = f(Z)$.

In the discrete case, conditional expectations are random variables that assume a constant value on each set of finite partitions. As the probability of these sets will not be zero, the values of conditional expectations are computed with the standard concept of conditional probability.

A.2.2 STOCHASTIC CALCULUS AND RISK NEUTRALIZATION

Much of the mathematics of modern finance theory depends on stochastic calculus. Stochastic calculus is the mathematical theory of those continuous-time stochastic processes that can be described through an instantaneous drift and an instantaneous volatility. These processes appear in a vast number of problems in scientific disciplines as diverse as physics, biology, and economics. Intuitively, they represent problems characterized by an instantaneous rate of growth (the drift term), plus some added random error term (the volatility term).

These processes were studied by the mathematician Ito, hence the name *Ito processes*. Suppose that a filtered probability space $(\Omega, \mathbf{F}, \{\mathbf{F}_t\}, P)$ is given. An Ito process is a stochastic process X_i characterized as:

$$X_t = x + \int_0^t \mu_s ds + \int_0^t \sigma_s dB_s$$

in integral notation and:

$$dX_t = \mu_t \, dt + \sigma_t \, dB_t$$

in differential notation.

In the most general case, μ_t and σ_t will be adapted stochastic processes that might be a function of X itself as well as of time, and B_t is a standard Brownian motion. Though widely used, the differential notation is really only another way of writing the integral equation.

If the processes μ_t and σ_t depend explicitly on the process X, the previous equation is called a stochastic differential equation (SDE) of the type:

$$dX_t = \mu_t(t, X_t)dt + \sigma_t(t, X_t)dB_t$$

in differential notation.

Before describing the processes themselves, it is appropriate to note that, as a mathematical object, an Ito process can be thought of as *the set of all continuous functions, eventually subject to additional mathematical constraints, starting at x over the time interval* [0,T]. Each continuous function is called a *path*. The mathematical description of the process is a way of assigning probabilities to the events of the probability space of which the paths are the outcomes. Processes differ only in the probability assignments, not in the paths.

In the above description of Ito processes, two terms appear under the integral sign. The first,

$$\int_0^t \mu_s ds$$

is the time integral of each path. It is clearly a time-dependent random variable, i.e., a stochastic process. The second term, however, is a different mathematical object, called a *stochastic integral*.

The definition of stochastic integrals is quite complex and proceeds in several steps. It begins with the definition of *Brownian motion* as the fundamental source of uncertainty. A Brownian motion (starting at zero) is a stochastic process $B_t = B(t)$ that respects the following conditions:

- $P(B_0 = 0) = 1$;
- For any instants t and s, $t > s$, the increments $B_s - B_t$ are normally distributed with expected value 0 and variance $t - s$;
- For any set of instants $t_0,...,t_n$ such that $0 < t_0 < t_1 < ... < t_n$, the corresponding random variables B_{t_i} are independent;
- For every $\omega \in \Omega$, the sample path $f(t) = B(\omega,t)$ is continuous.

It is possible to show that Brownian motion actually exists as a mathematical object, i.e., it is possible to construct a Brownian motion.

An adapted process θ_t is called "simple" if there is a partition of the interval $[0,T]$ given by the instants $0 = t_0 < t_1 < ... < t_n = T$ such that $\theta_t = \theta_{tn}$ for $t \in (t_{n-1}, t_n)$. For any simple adapted process q_t, the stochastic integral is defined as:

$$\int_0^T \theta_t dB_t = \Sigma \theta(t_i)[B(t_{i+1}) - B(t_i)] + \theta(t_n)[B(t) - B(t_n)].$$

It is also possible to show that, given any square integrable adapted process θ (not necessarily simple), there is a sequence of simple adapted processes θ_n that converges to θ in the sense that:

$$E\left(\int_0^T [\theta_n(t) - \theta(t)]^2 dt\right) \Rightarrow 0.$$

Finally, it is possible to show that, given any square integrable adapted process θ (not necessarily simple), there is a unique random variable Y_θ such that:

$$E\left(\left[Y_\theta - \int_0^T \theta_n(t) dB_t\right]^2\right) \Rightarrow 0.$$

This unique random variable Y_θ defines the stochastic integral:

$$Y_\theta = \int_0^T \theta_t dBt.$$

Ito processes have the property that any function of an Ito process is itself an Ito process. The *Ito lemma*, the key formula of stochastic calculus, prescribes conditions on the drift and volatility of derived processes.

The Ito lemma is stated as follows. Suppose that X_t is an Ito process defined as: $dX = \mu dt + \sigma dB$, with μ, σ, and B defined as in the previous paragraph. Suppose that $f(x,y)$ is a function of two variables with continuous partial derivatives, written as $f_y, f_{xx}, f_{yy}, f_{xy}, f_{yx}$. Then the process $Y_t = f(X_t, t)$ is an Ito process written as:

$$dY_t = (f_x(X_t, t)\mu + f_t(X_t, t) + \tfrac{1}{2}f_{tt}(X_t, t)\sigma_t^2)dt + f_x(X_t, t)\sigma_t dB_t.$$

The Ito lemma plays an important role in the demonstration of the Black-Scholes formula. It is also an important tool for deriving solutions to stochastic differential equations as defined above.

It is possible to show that a stochastic differential equation has a unique solution in the sense that it uniquely defines an Ito stochastic process. Recall the observation that Ito processes are the set of all continuous functions that begin at a given point x and that the previous formulas are ways of describing probability assignments over the space of these paths. While a deterministic differential equation defines a single path through time, a stochastic differential equation prescribes probabilities for all possible paths.

An important tool of stochastic calculus is the ability to change the description of an Ito process, simultaneously changing the probability measure P of the original probability space. It is possible to show that, by replacing the probability measure P with another equivalent probability measure Q (equivalence means that both P and Q assume value zero on the same sets) and the Brownian motion B with another Brownian motion B^*, any Ito process can be transformed into an Ito process of arbitrary drift. This is the essence of the Girsanov theorem. Processes must respect mathematical conditions (not given here) to ensure the applicability of the theorem.

The importance of the Girsanov theorem lies in the fact that it is possible to show that in the absence of arbitrage there is an equivalent probability measure Q such that, under Q, all price processes have drift equal to the instantaneous interest rate. In this equivalent martingale measure, all price processes discounted by the instantaneous interest rate are martingales, i.e., processes where the conditional expectation at future instants equals the present value.

This analysis, developed by Harrison and Kreps (1979) and Harrison and Pliska (1981), is central to modern finance theory and to modern risk management insofar as it enables a basic process of *risk neutralization*. In fact, it allows to perform all calculations as if they were processes in a risk-neutral world.

References

Harrison, J.M. and D. Kreps, "Martingales and Arbitrage in Multiperiod Securities Markets," *Journal of Economic Theory*, 20:381-408, 1979.

Harrison, J.M. and S. Pliska, "Martingales and Stochastic Integrals in the Theory of Continuous Trading," *Stochastic Processes and Their Applications*, 11:215-260, 1981.

A.2.3 THE NO-ARBITRAGE PRINCIPLE

By requiring that no trading strategy yield a sure profit with a zero-initial investment, the no-arbitrage principle prescribes basic consistency conditions between prices. A precise definition of the no-arbitrage principle depends on the representation considered.

The no-arbitrage principle is easy to state in the finite case. Consider a finite probability space (Ω, F, P) equipped with a filtration made up of $T+1$ algebras F_t corresponding to the $T+1$ instants from $t = 0$ to $t = T$. Suppose that there are n securities defined by the price and dividend adapted stochastic processes S_{i_t} and d_{i_t}, $i = 1,n$. A trading strategy θ_t is formed by n adapted processes θ_{i_t}, $i = 1,n$ that represent the quantity of each security held at instant t. It is assumed that there is no impediment to trading and that *short selling* is admitted. Portfolios might then assume any value, positive, zero, or negative.

The value of a trading strategy θ_t at instant t is:

$$S_{\theta_t} = \Sigma S_{i_t} \theta_{i_t} = S_t \theta_t$$

where the last quantity is a scalar product. The dividend process generated by a trading strategy is defined as

$$d_{\theta_t} = \theta_{t-1}(S_t + d_t) - \theta_t S_t.$$

Dividends can be positive, zero, or negative. The first dividend is simply the amount of the initial purchase. In the finite case, the no-arbitrage principle can be stated as follows: there is no trading strategy whose dividend process is never negative and is positive in some instant and for some state.

Defining the no-arbitrage principle in the continuous case, however, requires the specification of stochastic processes and gains. Suppose that a filtered probability space (Ω, F, P) is given and that the price processes *cum dividendi* is given by n Ito processes S_{i_t}, $i = 1,n$ where each S_{i_t} is written as:

$$S_{i_t} = x_i + \int_0^t \mu_{i_s} ds + \int_0^t \sigma_{i_s} dB_{i_s}$$

in integral notation and:

$$dS_{i_t} = \mu_{i_t} dt + \sigma_{i_t} dB_{i_t}$$

in differential notation.

A trading strategy is defined — as in the finite case — as a set of adapted processes that prescribe the quantity of each security held at each instant. The gain of a trading strategy θ_t is defined as the stochastic integral

$$\int_0^t \theta_t dS_t$$

defined as the Ito process:

$$\int_0^t \theta_t dS_t = \int_0^t \theta_t \mu_t dt + \int_0^t \theta_t \sigma_t dB_t$$

where the quantities under the integral are scalar products. A trading strategy: $\theta_t = (\theta_{1_t}, ..., \theta_{n_t})$ is called self-financing if:

$$\theta_t S_t = \theta_0 S_0 + \int_0^t \theta_t dS_t.$$

The condition of self-financing means that there is no inflow or outflow of money.

The no-arbitrage condition requires that, given any self-financing trading strategy, the conditions: $\theta_0 S_0 \leq 0$ and $\theta_t S_t > 0$ or $\theta_0 S_0 < 0$ and $\theta_t S_t \geq 0$ never happen.

These definitions can be further generalized to cover dividend price processes that include discontinuous processes and/or an infinite number of securities. These extensions present many mathematical subtleties. (See Delbaen and Schachermayer, 1994.)

References
Delbaen, Freddy and Walter Schachermayer, "A General Version of the Fundamental Theorem of Asset Pricing," *Mathematische Annalen*, 300,463-520, 1994.

A.2.4 FACTOR ANALYSIS

Factor analysis is a methodology for understanding and modeling the functional dependency of a set of random variables or stochastic processes on another set of random variables or stochastic processes called *factors*. By discovering functional relationships, the dimensionality of the stochastic description of phenomena might be significantly reduced. The challenge in factor analysis consists in finding a parsimonious set of factors that explains the empirical data.

One approach to factor analysis is theory building, i.e., establishing theoretical links between variables. Suppose that a set of phenomena is characterized by an ensemble of variables and that our objective is to ascertain the links between these variables so as to make all variables depend on or coincide with a smaller set of independent factors. There might be theoretical reasons that suggest a choice of factors and possible functional dependencies. In analyzing stock returns, for instance, there might be specific economic reasons for choosing some set of factors, e.g., macroeconomic variables responsible for a stock's returns.

A fairly complete mathematical methodology is available in the case of linear approximations. Suppose that a set of random variables $X_j, j = 1,N$ is given and that a set of factors $Z_i, i = 1,M$ have been identified. The objective is to establish a functional link of the type: $X_j = F_j(Z_1,...,Z_M, error\ terms)$ where the error terms are small.

If such a relationship can be established, then the value of X_j can be predicted from the value of the Z_i. Regression models are used in describing the functional dependence of a random variable X on one or more variables. A *regression function* is the representation of the conditional expectation $E(X/Z_1,...,Z_M)$ in function of the value of the conditioning variables, i.e., $E(X/Z_1,...,Z_M) = F(Z_1,...,Z_M)$.

A significant simplification is obtained if it is possible to approximate the function F with a linear relationship and if the residual is an independent white noise. In this case, we could write: $X = \sum \alpha_i Z_i + \beta + \varepsilon$ where α_i and β are constant and ε is a white noise. As a consequence, we could also write $E(X/Z_1,...,Z_M) = \sum \alpha_i Z_i + \beta$. Standard methods allow to estimate the coefficients α_i and β. If linear relationships are a good approximation of conditional expectations and if residuals are small, linear regression models provide useful insight.

The possibility of writing a factorization of this type depends on the problem under consideration and the choice of factors. Suppose that a portfolio is composed of a large number of securities whose returns are X_j. Whether returns can be expressed approximately as a linear combination of factors F_i such that $X_j = \sum \alpha_{ij} F_i + \varepsilon_j$ is an empirical problem.

Another approach is to apply mathematical methods to reduce the complexity of the stochastic description of phenomena. Suppose that a large set of random variables is given. In many cases, the objective is to reduce the size of the stochastic description. A portfolio of stocks, for instance, is described by the set of individual returns and their joint distribution. To optimize the portfolio's composition, it is mathematically convenient to express returns in function of a reduced number of factors. In the absence of theory, it is possible to attempt factor analysis, constructing abstract factors.

There are mathematical methods for identifying factors, though an economic interpretation must be given to factors heretofore only abstractly defined. Suppose that a set of jointly normal random variables X_i is given. These variables will be characterized by a potentially very large variance-covariance matrix. Under the assumption of joint normality, the variance-covariance matrix is sufficient to completely identify the given set of variables as well as any linear combination of them.

The objective is to find a reduced set of factors that are linear combinations of the X_is. One methodology for building factors, *principal component analysis* (PCA), consists in computing the eigenvectors $\beta_j = (\beta_{j1},...,\beta_{jN})^T$ and the corresponding eigenvalues λ_j of the variance-covariance matrix $\mathbf{R} = [\sigma_{ij}]$, $i = 1,N$, $j = 1,N$ so that: $\mathbf{R}\beta_j = \lambda_j \beta_j$. Eigenvectors generate orthogonal factors B_j as linear combinations of the X_is: $B_i = \sum \alpha_{ij} X_j$. Each factor is a normal variable whose variance is the corresponding eigenvalue.

Suppose that eigenvalues are arranged in decreasing order: $\lambda_1 > \lambda_j > \lambda_N$. If the first M factors have variances much larger than the others, it is possible to express each original variable as a linear combination of a reduced number M of factors plus an error term. If error terms are small, factorization is successful. This methodology can be used when a variance-covariance matrix describes a process.

Yet another approach is to start from a set of multidimensional observations without any prior explanatory hypotheses. The problem here consists in modeling variables and distributions that account for the random variation in data. The objective is to find a parsimonious explanation that would allow to reduce uncertainty by performing only a limited set of measurements. One starts by determining the plane along which the data present the maximum variance and then repeats the process for orthogonal planes. A set of orthogonal factors is thereby identified. Figure A.2.4.1 illustrates how principal component analysis identifies the directions of maximum variance; factors follow these directions.

Figure A.2.4.1
Factors A and B follow the directions of maximum variance.

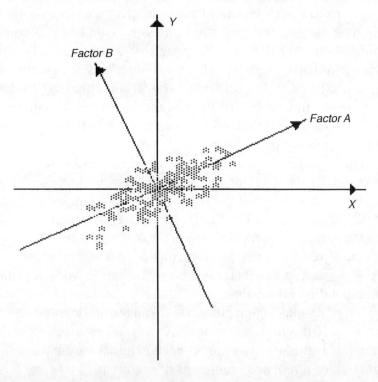

In the above, the assumption of linearity and normality plays a fundamental role. The nonlinear case is more difficult to handle from the point of view of both theory and statistics. Nonlinear methodologies such as segmentation algorithms, neural networks, Kohonen maps, and induction trees are now being used to perform statistical factor analysis in the nonlinear case.

Nonlinear methodologies might start from raw data to identify the most significant segments of data to be used as factors. Or they can work on preprocessed data and distributions. These methodologies belong to the field of data mining. Complex nonlinear problems will generally require a combination of theoretical insight and statistical analysis.

The notion of factor analysis is not limited to sets of random variables, but might involve stochastic processes. As in the above cases, the starting point can be either sets of empirical time series or sets of stochastic processes. The objective is to determine the best, most parsimonious representation of the processes. One might, for instance, cluster a set of sample processes to find representatives for each cluster. Again, a combination of theory and statistical analysis will be required.

A.2.5 THE THEORY OF FORECASTING

To forecast is to compute a probability distribution at some future instant or sets of instants given present and past events. It may prove impossible to compute explicitly the entire probability distributions. In this case, only point forecasts, i.e., single values that represent our best estimate of the quantities to be forecast, can be computed. Domain-specific theories entail forecasts. Physics, for example, entails the ability to forecast physical phenomena. The theory of forecasting identifies methodologies for arriving at optimal forecasts, even in the absence of firm domain-specific theories.

The notion of point forecasts can be expressed by the notion of the *data generating process* (DGP) of a time series. The DGP of a series is the mathematical relationship that links the value of a time series at instant t with its values in previous instants. It takes its name from its ability, as a mathematical algorithm, to *generate* a series from initial data. Consider a time series in discrete time: $x(t_i)$, $i = 1,N$. The DGP of this series will be an equation of the form: $x(t_i) = f(x(t_{i-1}),...,x(t_{i-m}))$. This equation represents the functional link between the value of the time series at any given point with the values in the m previous points. Figure A.2.5.1 illustrates the DGP as a multivariate function.

The DGP generalizes to cover the case where each of a set of time series depends on other time series in the same set. Formally, we can write the previous relationship in vector form: $x(t_i) = f(x(t_{i-1}),...,x(t_{i-m}))$ where $x(t_i) = (x_1(t_i),...,x_p(t_i))$ is a p-component vector and the function f is a set of p functions f_j, $j = 1,p$. In some cases, the function f might be the explicit representation of the solution of a system of equations that link the values of the time series in different points.

The representation of a DGP is more general than it might at first appear. Data points might include not only original raw data but also derived variables obtained through operations such as differencing or detrending. Differential equations, for instance, are often approximated by difference equations that can be expressed as a function: $x(t_i) = f(x(t_{i-1}),...,x(t_{i-m}))$. A time series which is the discretized version of a continuous function subject to integro-differential equations and initial conditions will, in general, admit a DGP.

Figure A.2.5.1

The data generating process (DGP) of a time series is the function that expresses the link between successive points in the series.

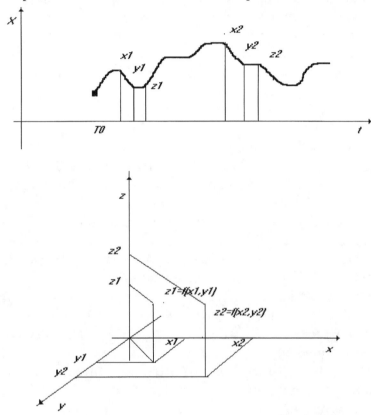

The problem of the theory of forecasting is to determine the best DGP given a set of points of a time series. This is a problem of generalization: the fundamental relationship between successive points is known in a number of past cases; the objective is to generalize to the entire time series. There are a number of algorithms and optimality criteria for performing generalization.

In the absence of a firm theory of the phenomena under study, forecasting methodologies assume that the DGP has some predefined functional form containing free parameters. The forecasting algorithms determine the parameters through a learning process. The many different learning algorithms, including neural networks, work by optimizing functions that represent the cost of deviation from the training data.

Now frequently used in forecasting, neural networks learn the relationship $x(t_i) = f(x(t_{i-1}),...,x(t_{i-m}))$. The network implements an expansion in a truncated series of functions; the weights of the network are the free parameters that are optimized through learning procedures such as backpropagation.

As the problem of generalization lacks a comprehensive solution, the existence of a generating function for a time series is not guaranteed. There might be time series that cannot be described by any program shorter that the enumeration of the series itself. (See Chaitin, 1987, for an exploration of the theory of algorithmic complexity and Wolpert, 1995, for an exposition of the theory of generalization.) In addition, the DGP of a series might simply be too complex to allow for learning by samples within an acceptable time-frame. Methods of nonlinear dynamics might help in ascertaining the complexity of the DGP of a given empirical series.

The DGP determined by a forecasting procedure will, in general, be only approximate and subject to error. The approximate and uncertain nature of forecasting should be noted: misunderstandings over forecasting and its applicability to finance can derive from losing sight of the fact that forecasts are only approximate and carry uncertainty. It would, of course, be interesting to be able to determine the size of the forecasting error but, in general, this can only be estimated through statistical methods.

Uncertainty can be handled upfront. In fact, the notion of point forecasts can be extended to cover the case of probabilistic forecasts. In this case, it is not the relationships between single points but those between successive probability distributions that are considered. There are different methodologies for probabilistic forecasting. The simplest is to assume that the value of a time series at each instant is a random variable. The DGP becomes a functional relationship between random variables.

Forecasts are *conditional*. In fact, if $X(t_i)$ is a random variable that represents a time series at instant t_i, the DGP will have an expression of the form: $X(t_i) = G(X(t_{i-1}),...,X(t_{i-j}),random\ error\ terms)$. This expression is a functional link between random variables and prespecified random error terms such as white noise. With this function, it is possible to compute the conditional expectation of $X(t_i)$ given known past values of the time series: $E(X(t_i)/X(t_{i-1}),...,X(t_{i-j})) = F(X(t_{i-1}),...,X(t_{i-j}))$. The function F might not coincide with the function G.

Examples of these methodologies are the Auto Regressive (AR), the Moving Average (MA), and the Auto Regressive Moving Average (ARMA) models of time series. The AR model posits a linear autoregressive relationship of the form: $X_t = \sum \alpha_j X_{t-j} + \varepsilon_t$, where ε_t is a zero-mean white noise. The MA model posits a linear relationship of the form: $X_t = \sum \beta_j \varepsilon_{t-j}$, where ε_{t-j}, is a zero-mean white noise. The ARMA model posits a relationship which is a sum of the above: $X_t = \sum \alpha_j X_{t-j}, + \sum \beta_j \varepsilon_{t-j}$. Nonlinear models include the ARCH and GARCH models of volatility.

The forecasting problem consists in determining the unknown parameters in the chosen model. This can be achieved through various learning and optimization procedures. The Box-Jenkins methodology is frequently used in the linear case; for the nonlinear case, a number of models and learning algorithms such as quadratic regression can be used.

A different mathematical model is obtained by describing the probability distributions of values conditional on some past event. Examples include Markov chains. Markov chains describe time series that can assume only a finite number N of values and that are characterized by an $N \times N$ transition probability matrix $[P_{ij}]$. The matrix $[P_{ij}]$ prescribes the probability of each of the N possible values at time t given any of the same n possible values at time $t-1$. In this case, the forecasting problem is the statistical estimate of the transition matrix. An example is the estimate of the transition probability matrix of credit ratings.

The notion of a generating mechanism of a time series generalizes to stochastic processes in continuous time. One has, however, to replace the functional relationships between adjacent points with continuous-time relationships that define stochastic processes. There are different ways to tackle this problem. One might specify upfront the finite joint distributions of stochastic processes; one might use the notions and tools of stochastic calculus, namely stochastic differential equations; or one might consider differential equations that constrain the evolution of conditional probability distributions, such as the Fokker-Planck equation.

Descriptions of stochastic processes in continuous time are forecasts of the most general type. Continuous-time forecasting methodologies consist in estimating a number of parameters that define continuous processes. Assuming, for instance, a geometrical Brownian motion as the generalized process, its drifts and volatilities must be estimated.

It should be remarked that the notion of forecasting is not limited to sure deterministic predictions but encompasses any mechanism that prescribes the stochastic evolution of a time series in discrete or continuous time. In finance theory and in economics, forecasting relationships are approximate and probabilistic: forecasts are therefore subject to uncertainty and error.

References

Chaitin, Gregory J., *Algorithmic Information Theory*, Cambridge University Press, New York, NY, 1987.

Wolpert, David H., editor, *The Mathematics of Generalization*, Proceedings vol. XX, Santa Fe Institute, Studies in the Sciences of Complexity, Addison-Wesley, Reading, MA, 1995.

A.2.6 DATA-MINING TECHNIQUES

Data mining is a set of mathematical methods for discovering relationships hidden in vast sets of data. A mathematical model of the data is built using a process of "learning," the fundamental notion of data mining. Machine-learning techniques can be divided into two types: *supervised learning* and *unsupervised learning*. (See Figure A.2.6.1 for a summary of the respective functions and techniques.)

Supervised learning is learning from examples. The end product of supervised learning is a classifier which assigns a classification value to each individual in a set. As individuals are identified by variables, a classifier is a function from a set of variables into a set of classification values.

Suppose that a set of data samples of M individuals is given. These sample data $(y_i;x_{i1},...,x_{iN})$, $i = 1,M$ will include the values of the N variables $x_{i1},...,x_{iN}$ that identify each individual as well as their corresponding classification values y_i. The set of sample data is called the *training set*. Learning algorithms attempt to find a function y: $F(x_1,...,x_N)$ able to reproduce, in some optimal way, the M data samples. There are many learning schemes. Each consists in minimizing some function of the differences between the sample points and the computed points plus, eventually, some additional theoretical term.

Neural networks and induction trees are the better known of the supervised learning schemes. Available in a wide range of topologies, neural networks attempt to learn a function by expanding it in a truncated series of special functions and determining the expansion coefficients through procedures such as backpropagation. Induction trees attempt to identify, in some optimal way, the regions over which a function can be represented by a constant value and to determine the values for each region.

The critical issue in supervised learning is generalization. The objective of learning is not to reproduce with the highest possible accuracy the given samples, but to come as close as possible to points outside of the learning set. Suppose that classification data are generated by some *true function* $y = G(x_1,...,x_N)$. We know only a sample set of realizations of that function given by the samples $(y_i;x_{i1},...,x_{iN})$. The objective of learning is to make F as close as possible to G over its entire domain. Formulating a theory of generalization is not easy: every theory makes limiting assumptions on the possible sets of true functions G. (See Wolpert, 1995.)

The effectiveness of learning and of learning schemes is an empirical question. A number of practical problems lend themselves to learning; others are too complex in the sense that the classification function, if it exists at all, would require an inordinately large number of samples. There is no guarantee that a classification problem can be solved with reasonably simple functions.

Unsupervised learning is more difficult to define theoretically. In unsupervised learning, a system evolves following its own dynamics. There is no training set; algorithms might work on the entire set of data. In intuitive terms, unsupervised learning gives explicit form to some implicit description of data. From the point of view of risk management, the most important unsupervised learning schemes are clustering and segmentation. These schemes identify typical individuals or sets of individuals that share some common feature(s). They are nonlinear insofar as the boundary of the segments can be defined by nonlinear functions.

Segmentation divides a set of individuals into classes that are maximally homogeneous with respect to some measure of the "distance" between individuals. Clustering is a similar function: it groups together individuals around some typical individual. There are many different algorithms for segmentation and clustering. Among them, Kohonen maps and similarity maximization algorithms are the most widely used.

Figure A.2.6.1.
**Learning schemes and their typical functions
and implementation techniques.**

Learning schemes	Functions	Techniques
Supervised learning	Classification	Neural networks Induction trees
Unsupervised learning	Clustering Segmentation	Kohonen maps Similarity maximization

An oft-asked question is: What is the relationship between data mining and statistics? Data-mining algorithms are *deterministic* algorithms that entail an approximation error. As such, they can be given a statistical *interpretation*. For example, neural networks — though a deterministic approximation algorithm — can be described within a statistical mechanics framework (see Hertz, Krogh, and Palmer, 1991).

References

Hertz, John, Anders Krogh, and Richard Palmer, *Introduction to the Theory of Neural Computation*, Addison Wesley, Redwood, CA, 1991.

Wolpert, David H., editor, *The Mathematics of Generalization*, Proceedings vol. XX, Santa Fe Institute, Studies in the Sciences of Complexity, Addison-Wesley, Reading, MA, 1995.

A.2.7 TERM-STRUCTURE MODELS

At every instant, there is an entire curve of interest rates. In fact, at time t, it is necessary to consider not only the instantaneous interest rate at that instant but also the interest rates implied by the price of zero-coupon risk-free bonds of various maturities. The set of these interest rates for all possible maturities is called the term structure of interest rates. The latter might be given different equivalent representations, such as the curve of discount factors, i.e., the price of nominal bonds, or the curve of the yields to maturity of bonds.

There are different frameworks for modeling interest rates. Each is characterized by those processes that are taken as a given and by the probability settings adopted. One might take as a given the short rate or the price of a set of securities such as risk-free bonds that determine the term structure. Other possible choices include the forward Libor and swap rates. The usual equivalent martingale measure can be replaced by other probability transformations such as forward measures.

The most commonly used framework considers as a given the short-rate process $r(t)$ and assumes a suitable model for that process in the risk-neutral world, i.e., under an equivalent martingale measure. Consider *single-factor short-rate models*. Suppose that Q is an equivalent martingale measure and that B^* is a standard Brownian motion under Q. Single-factor models assume that the short-rate $r_t \equiv r(t)$ follows an Ito diffusion of the form:

$$dr_t = \mu(r_t, t)dt + \sigma(r_t, t)dB_t^*$$

in the equivalent martingale measure Q.

Given this process, the term structure can be derived. In fact, it is possible to show that, in the equivalent martingale measure Q, the term structure $\Lambda_{t,T}$, i.e., the price at time t of a zero-coupon risk-free bond maturing at T, follows the process:

$$\Lambda_{t,T} = E_t^Q\left[\exp\left(-\int_t^T r_s ds\right)\right].$$

In addition, the Feynman-Kac approach to the solution of stochastic equations implies that $\Lambda_{t,T} = f(r_t,t)$ where the function $f(x,t)$ must satisfy the Feynman-Kac equation:

$$\mathbf{D}f(x, t) - xf(x, t) = 0$$

with boundary conditions $f(x,T) = 1$, where:

$$\mathbf{D}f(x, t) = f_t(x, t) + f_x(x, t)\mu(x, t) + \tfrac{1}{2}f_{xx}(x, t)\sigma(x, t)^2$$

and where f_t, f_x, f_{xx} represent partial derivatives. The above framework has been specialized through different choices of the short-rate process, originating a wide class of models which includes the Cox-Ingersoll-Ross and Vasicek models. There are important modeling questions in the choice of specific processes, e.g., interest rates cannot become negative and tend to stay within some long-term band (mean reversion).

The above reasoning can be extended to cover *multifactor models*. In the multifactor case, a set of factor processes is given under the equivalent martingale measure. Consider an equivalent martingale measure Q and an N-dimensional standard Brownian motion B_t^* under Q. Suppose that factors X_t are represented by Ito diffusions of the type:

$$dX_t = \mu(X_t, t)dt + \sigma(X_t, t)dB_t^*$$

and that the short rate is represented by an Ito process of the type: $r_t = R(X_t,t)$. The term structure can be determined following the same approach as in the single-factor case.

By appropriately choosing the free parameters, it is generally possible to fit approximately the present term structure. The lack of an exact fit might, however, be a problem. *No-arbitrage interest rate models* make it possible to fit exactly the present observed term structure.

The no-arbitrage framework for interest rates takes as a given the underlying bond price processes and derives the various rates from these processes. In this way, the present term structure is automatically respected. To illustrate how this method works, suppose that, given an equivalent martingale measure Q and a standard Brownian process $B_t{}^*$ under Q, the price process at time t of a zero-coupon risk-free bond maturing at T, $\Lambda_{t,T} = \Lambda(t,T)$ follows a process of the type:

$$d\Lambda = r(t)\Lambda dt + v(t, T)\Lambda dB_t{}^*.$$

It can be shown that this process determines the short-rate process which can be explicitly written as an Ito process:

$$r(t) = \Lambda(0, t) + \int_0^t vv_t ds + \int_0^t v_t dB_t{}^*.$$

The short-rate process can also be written as:

$$dr(t) = \Lambda(0, t) + \left[\int_0^t (vv_t + v_{tt}^2)ds\right]dt + \int_0^t [v_{tt}dB_t{}^*]dt + v_t dB_t{}^*.$$

This methodology can be generalized to cover multiple factors and more general price processes. A number of arbitrage-free interest-rate models have been proposed, including the Ho-Lee and Hull-White models. The Ho-Lee model has the form:

$$dr(t) = \theta(t)dt + \sigma dB_t{}^*.$$

The Hull-White model has the form:

$$dr(t) = [\theta(t) - \alpha r(t)]dt + \sigma dB_t{}^*.$$

In some instances, it might be more convenient to express bond prices in terms of the forward rates. An important question, from a conceptual and practical point of view, is what conditions on the instantaneous forward rate processes make the processes coherent with an arbitrage-free system of bond prices. The Heath-Jarrow-Morton methodology addresses this question. It assumes that the instantaneous forward rates $F(t,T)$ follow an Ito process of the form:

$$dF = \mu dt + \sigma dB_t{}^*$$

and shows that, in order to obtain arbitrage-free bond price processes, the drift and volatility μ, σ must respect the conditions:

$$\mu(t, T) = \sigma(t, T)\int_t^T \sigma(t, s)ds.$$

A different approach was taken by Marek Musiela and developed by Farshid Jamshidian. Jamshidian observed that models of interest rates based on continuously compounding instantaneous rates contradict common practices such as the monthly accrual method of Libor rates. To solve this and other problems related to trading practices, Jamshidian developed the theory of Libor and swap rates. Instead of the usual equivalent martingale measure, this approach uses a probability measure given by forward swap or forward Libor rates.

Jamshidian (1996) represents forward Libor or swap rates by a system of stochastic differential equations, with one equation corresponding to each payment reset date. Libor rates, for example, are represented by a set of stochastic processes L_n. Each L_n, which corresponds to a reset date, is represented as an Ito process in the forward Libor measure. This representation makes interest rates compatible with the discrete sequence of Libor payment dates and with trading practices such as the widely used Black-Scholes formula.

References

Jamshidian, Farshid, "Libor and Swap Market Models and Measures," Sakura Global Capital, January 1996.

A.3.1 SIMULATION AND DIFFERENTIAL EQUATIONS

The numerical methods used in risk management depend on the underlying mathematical approach and, in particular, on the description of stochastic processes. There are two major frameworks for describing stochastic processes. One is stochastic calculus, an approach that models stochastic processes upfront by considering the fundamental sources of uncertainty provided by Brownian motions. The second uses partial differential equations to model the *deterministic* evolution of probability distributions.

The stochastic calculus approach leads to simulation and Monte Carlo methods. In fact, this approach describes stochastic processes through stochastic integration based on Brownian motion. It employs a set of methods that translate into simulating paths of stochastic processes starting from sources of randomness typically provided by the generation of random numbers.

From a numerical point of view, simulation might be quite onerous. Monte Carlo methods, for instance, might rapidly become too time-consuming when considering a large number of scenarios. A major effort is under way to develop techniques to reduce the number of paths to be simulated.

At Sakura Global Capital, Farshid Jamshidian and Yu Zhu (1997) used the tools of factor analysis in developing their Scenario Simulation methodology. This model represents interest rates by a set of key rates that are assumed to be lognormally distributed as each rate is described by a geometric Brownian motion. Suppose that there are N key rates and that the correlation between different key rates is described by a variance-covariance matrix $\mathbf{R} = [\sigma_{ij}]$, $i = 1,N$, $j = 1,N$. This is an N-factor model.

A complete Monte Carlo simulation would imply the consideration of the full variance-covariance matrix of the distribution of key rates, resulting in a problem of excessive computational complexity. To reduce the dimensionality of the problem, Jamshidian and Zhu use the technique of principal component analysis. To this end, the eigenvectors β_j and the corresponding eigenvalues λ_j of the matrix $\mathbf{R}$ are computed so that: $\mathbf{R}\beta_j = \lambda_j \beta_j$. It can be demonstrated empirically that the first three eigenvalues are much larger than the others, which can therefore be ignored. The interest-rate model is then reduced to a three-factor model. This reduction corresponds to taking into account only the parallel shifts, bends, and butterfly twists of the curve.

Another method — the Linear Path Space (LPS) — was developed by GAT president Thomas Ho (1992). The problem is the same as above, i.e., sampling the set of interest-rate paths in an effort to reduce the number of paths to be simulated. LPS solves the problem by clustering paths, i.e., by segmenting the path space into equivalence classes based on a notion of "distance" between paths. After performing the clustering function, a representative from each cluster is sampled.

The differential-equations approach uses a number of mathematical results that link stochastic equations to partial differential equations. A rich mathematical theory shows how solutions of differential equations can be expressed as expected values of corresponding stochastic processes. Conversely, solutions of stochastic equations correspond to differential equations that model the evolution of transition probability distributions. Generally speaking, a differential operator is associated with each stochastic equation. Ito diffusions, for example, are associated with the Kolmogorov and Fokker-Planck equations, both well known in statistical physics.

A vast set of numerical methods exist for solving partial differential equations. These methods are based on a process of discretization that transforms the original differential equation into a set of algebraic equations. They are widely used in the physical sciences where the solution of differential equations is standard methodology.

References

Ho, Thomas S.Y., "Managing Illiquid Bonds and the Linear Path Space," *The Journal of Fixed Income*, vol. 2, no. 1, June 1992.

Jamshidian, Farshid and Yu Zhu, "Scenario Simulation: Theory and Methodology," *Finance and Stochastics* 1(1), 43-67, January 1997.

A.5.1 STOCHASTIC OPTIMIZATION

Deterministic optimization problems are generally formulated as the minimization or maximization of an objective function in a possible set of values given a set of constraints. Optimization problems are called programs; the corresponding solution is called linear programming if functions are linear, mathematical programming if objective functions are nonlinear.

If parameters are not known with certainty, optimization problems are called stochastic optimization programs and the solution technique *stochastic programming* or *stochastic optimization*. The optimization of portfolios of stocks is an example of optimization problems subject to uncertainty. A portfolio is optimized maximizing some utility function over a set of returns subject to uncertainty.

The solution of a stochastic optimization problem is achieved by defining a corresponding deterministic problem, the *deterministic equivalent*. If stock returns are assumed to be normal, a deterministic equivalent is given by maximizing utility functions defined over variances-covariances and expected values. This is the deterministic equivalent of the initial stochastic optimization problem.

Stochastic optimization problems are of special interest when decisions are made at intermediate points, taking into account future decisions. Each decision entails a set of conditional probabilities. Finding and solving a deterministic equivalent might prove difficult. In fact, it is possible to define the deterministic equivalent as the maximization of the expected value of the problem's objective function. But given the need to re-evaluate conditional probabilities at each future point, this could prove a computationally intractable task for time-dependent problems.

Various techniques have been proposed for solving multistage stochastic optimization. *Bellman's dynamic programming* uses a backward approach based on the Bellman optimality principle. This principle states that for any optimal policy and under appropriate conditions, decisions at any point must optimize the remaining section of the problem. The optimization problem is therefore processed backward, starting from the last set of decisions.

Scenario optimization is a different sort of approach. It considers uncertainties upfront, as a set of possible scenarios. A probability weight is associated to each scenario. Various implementation methods have been advanced, including Scenario Aggregation proposed by Rockafellar and Wets (1991), and Scenario Optimization proposed by Ron Dembo (1991) and implemented in the optimization software developed by Algorithmics.

References

Dembo, Ron S., "Scenario Optimization," *Annals of Operations Research*, vol. 30, 1991.

Rockafellar, R.T. and R.J.B. Wets, "Scenarios and Policy Aggregation in Optimization Under Uncertainty," *Math. Oper. Research*, 16: 119.147, 1991.

A.7.1 MARKET MICROSTRUCTURE THEORY

Market microstructure theory attempts to describe the price-formation process that results from trading. In principle, it marks a departure from one of the fundamental tenets of perfect markets: the price-taking behavior of agents. Neoclassical finance theory posits that agents are price-takers as they are individually too small to influence the market. Prices are fixed by a hypothetical agent optimization mechanism that reaches equilibrium.

In the neoclassical formulation, equilibrium is a mathematical concept that implies rational expectations. Mathematical utility maximization is the price-discovery or price-setting mechanism for determining prices; demand and supply are modeled through it. There is no concept of statistical equilibrium with possible fluctuations around some equilibrium state.

When modeling market microstructure, however, the question of price formation has to be considered upfront. Ultimately, there is the need to understand how trades characterized by a demand-and-supply schedule influence prices. This raises conceptual challenges.

Different theoretical approaches have been proposed. The first, beginning with Mark Garman (1976), uses *inventory models*. An inventory model posits a monopolistic market-maker as a liquidity provider. This agent sets the price at which he or she will buy or sell stocks and fill orders. The agent's objective is to optimize, avoiding bankruptcy (i.e., running out of cash) and failure to deliver (i.e., running out of stocks).

Inventory models assume that the monopolistic market-maker knows the stochastic process governing order arrival and sets prices in consequence. The analytical inventory problem has been solved under different assumptions (e.g., representations of the order arrival processes) and using different techniques. Eventually, the assumption of a monopolistic market-maker can be released, allowing for competing traders.

A more recent approach to market microstructure theory is based on *information models*. Rather than attempt to optimize inventory, market-makers are modeled as trading on the basis of information, optimizing their portfolios in function of their expectations and without cash limitations.

Both inventory and information models posit exogenous processes for order and information flows. Generally, these models do not take into consideration the feedback of prices on the order-arrival process. From the practical as well as conceptual point of view, however, it is interesting to understand how price information is fed back into the behavior of investors.

A radically different approach to market microstructure theory is based on *game theory*: every agent is engaged in a game with every other agent in the market; prices emerge in function of the mutual adjustment of agents. Though conceptually interesting, this approach runs into formidable computational difficulties. As a consequence, only small idealized "toy" markets have been fully analyzed.

More recent — and more promising — studies on market microstructure are based on notion of the market as a set of multiple interacting agents taken at some level of aggregation. In these models, the price formation process emerges from the dynamical laws of the market. The latter are derived from concepts of nonequilibrium *statistical mechanics*, including aggregation and market feedback phenomena. There is no exogenously given process; markets evolve as physical systems whose internal structure is known.

These new modeling approaches provide fundamental insight into how micro rules such as the learning behavior of agents are projected onto the behavior of statistical aggregates. These ideas are now finding their way into the theory of market microstructure and, more in general, into macroeconomics itself (see Aoki, 1996, and Kirman, 1997).

The Market Impact Model recently released by BARRA applies market microstructure theory to modeling the impact of trades on prices. It makes the realistic assumption that trading takes place in a competitive multiagent environment. The market is characterized through mathematical links between five key variables: the sensitivity of orders to price changes, trading volume, price volatility, trade size, and risk remuneration. Mathematical models, calibrated to market data, were built for various equity trading environments.

References

Aoki, Masanao, *New Approaches to Macroeconomic Modeling*, Cambridge University Press, New York, NY, 1996.

Garman, Mark, "Market Microstructure," *Journal of Financial Economics*, 3:257-275, 1976.

Kirman, Alan P., "The Market as an Interactive System," Working Paper, GREQAM, EHESS and the University of Aix-Marseille III, Marseille, 1997.

A.7.2 STATISTICAL MECHANICS

The concepts of statistical mechanics are being used in a new theoretical approach to economics and financial modeling. Finance theory might be affected. The starting point of a statistical mechanics approach is to view the economy as a multiagent system, i.e., a system made up of many interacting entities. The key insights are the modeling of aggregation phenomena and the contraction and projection of information at different levels of coarse graining.

Statistical mechanics is a set of mathematical methods from the domain of physics. Its development dates back to the end of the 19th century. The objective was to explain a number of macroscopic laws — mainly in the field of thermodynamics — as statistical averages of the motion of large sets of microscopic particles. As microscopic particles obey well known laws of mechanics, statistical physics was considered a major triumph of physics: it provides a unification of physical laws. During this century, and in particular in the last fifty years, statistical physics has provided not only additional conceptual consolidation but also fresh insight into many phenomena, especially in the domain of nonequilibrium statistical physics. (See Kubo, Toda, Hashitsume, 1991, for an advanced exposition of statistical physics.)

Methods of both equilibrium and nonequilibrium statistical physics solve different problem domains. The first is the modeling of phenomena through systems of stochastic differential equations and their associated partial differential equations. These methods prescribe how to introduce uncertainty and indeterminacy into deterministic equations. Ito diffusions are an example.

The underlying reasoning here is that it is possible to ascertain the deterministic evolution of probability distributions although individual behavior is uncertain. Mathematical methodologies include the description of stochastic processes either as stochastic equations such as Ito diffusions, or as deterministic equations for probability distributions such as the Fokker-Planck equation and the formalism of master equations.

The second domain of statistical physics is the projection of information onto different levels of aggregation. These methods are used in physics to describe the evolution of systems in the absence of detailed information on a number of variables. The microscopic laws are known, but detailed information on each microcomponent is missing. Methods such as those developed by Mori (1965) address these problems.

Statistical physics also provides mathematical methods for analyzing the aggregation of large sets of agents. This is perhaps the field that has received the most attention to date. It has been formalized in different contexts, among them synergetics, dissipative structures, and the maximum entropy formalism. A physical analogy to aggregation phenomena is provided by systems that move in a potential field that is influenced by the system's own dynamics, i.e., in self-referential systems. Millonas (1996) offers an overview of recent advances in the field of the evolution of complex structures.

Lastly, statistical concepts of equilibrium will provide new insight into economic equilibrium. In real economic life, equilibrium is of a statistical nature with gains continuously offsetting losses. This insight is particularly important in the notion of equilibrium in time, a notion missing in present economic theory. Risk is a case in point: risk management is ultimately the ability to reach a long-term statistical equilibrium of losses and gains.

References

Aoki, Masanao, *New Approaches to Macroeconomic Modeling*, Cambridge University Press, New York, NY, 1996.

Kubo, R., M. Toda and N. Hashitsume, *Statistical Physics II*, Springer-Verlag, Berlin, 1991.

Millonas, Mark, Editor, *Fluctuations and Order: The New Synthesis*, Springer-Verlag, New York, NY, 1996.

Mori, H., *Prog. Theor. Phys.*, 33:424+, 1965.

Index

Tools of the Trade

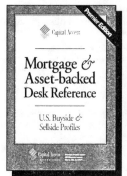  

Capital Access Desk Reference Series

☐ **Yes.** Please send me the following titles from the Capital Access Desk Reference Series.

Quantity	Title	Price Per Copy	Amount
	Corporate Bond Desk Reference	$395.⁰⁰	
	Mortgage & Asset-backed Desk Reference	$395.⁰⁰	
	Derivatives Desk Reference (Available 4th Quarter 1997)	$395.⁰⁰	
	Shipping & Handling: Within U.S.A. $8.50 Per Copy		
	*Outside U.S.A. $70.00 Per Copy		
	NJ Residents Add 6% Sales Tax		
	Total Amount		

☐ Check Enclosed ☐ Bill Me ☐ Visa ☐ Mastercard ☐ American Express

NAME: _____ TITLE: _____

COMPANY: _____

ADDRESS: _____ STATE: _____ ZIP CODE: _____

PHONE: _____ FAX: _____

ACCOUNT NUMBER: _____ EXPIRATION DATE: _____

PURCHASE ORDER NUMBER: _____ SIGNATURE: X _____

* All orders outside the U.S. must be prepaid in U.S. Dollars with funds drawn on a U.S. bank.

Three easy ways to order:

✓ **Fax:** (908) 771-0330   ✓ **Call:** (800) 866-5987   ✓ **Or mail** order form to:

Capital Access International • Mountain Heights Center 430 Mountain Avenue • Murray Hill, New Jersey 07974

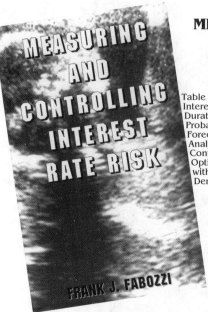

DICTIONARY OF FINANCIAL RISK MANAGEMENT

Gary L. Gastineau and Mark P. Kritzman
1996   Hardcover   307 Pages   Price $45
ISBN 1-883249-14-7

Risk management terminology comes by many markets
– cash, forwards/futures, swaps, options – and from
many disciplines – economics, probability and statistics,
tax and financial accounting, and law. The vocabulary of
the risk manager continues to expand with the creation
of new products and new concepts. All these words and
phrases are carefully defined and illustrated in this comprehensive dictionary.

About the authors: Gary L. Gastineau is Senior Vice
President, New Product Development at the American
Stock Exchange, an Adjunct Professor at The Center for
Technology and Financial Services at the Polytechnic
Institute, and an independent risk management consul-
tant. Mark P. Kritzman is the Managing Partner of
Windham Capital Management in Boston, which special-
izes in asset allocation and currency management.

MODELING THE MARKET: NEW THEORIES AND TECHNIQUES

MODELING THE MARKET: NEW THEORIES AND TECHNIQUES

Sergio Focardi & Caroline Jonas

Sergio Focardi and Caroline Jonas
1997 Hardcover 289 Pages Price $55
ISBN 1-883249-12-0

About the authors: Sergio Focardi is a partner of The Intertek Group. Caroline Jonas is a partner of The Intertek Group.

"(This) book looks at the progress made, both in practice and in theory, towards producing a usable model of the market. Some of the theoretical foundations of efficient market theory are being demolished." Philip Coggan, *Financial Times*

"... the authors have done an admirable job .. this book is a revealing and fascinating glimpse of the technologies which may rule the financial market in the years to come." Sumit Paul-Choudhury, *Risk*

To order books from Frank J. Fabozzi Associates, contact us:

- by fax: (215) 598-8932
- by phone: (215) 598-8930
- by mail: Frank J. Fabozzi Associates
            858 Tower View Circle, New Hope, PA 18938
- or visit our Web site: www.frankfabozzi.com